100 Years of
Nestlé Rowntree Band

1903 - 2003

First published 2005

Published by The Shepherd Building Group Brass Band

The Shepherd Building Group Brass Band,
Mrs. A Brown, Secretary,
54 Bad Bargain Lane,
York YO31 OQl

Printed and bound in England by:
York Publishing Services Limited,
64 Hallfield Road,
Layerthorpe,
York YO31 7ZQ

Contents

Acknowledgments

Foreword   1

Introduction   3

SECTION 1   1903 - 2003

Chapter

1.	5
2.	17
3.	27
4.	35
5.	43
6.	49
7.	55
8.	61
9.	73
10.	81
11.	89
12.	99
13.	107
14.	115
15.	127
16.	139
17.	147

SECTION 2   BEHIND THE STAND

Senior Band	155
Concert Band	179
Beginner's Band	193
Associate Members	199
Past Members	203

SECTION 3   IN CONCLUSION

Appendix	227
Thanks to Sharon Long	234
Into the Future	235

Acknowledgements

I would like to thank the following for their assistance
in the preparation of this book.

Mr Trevor Collins

Mr and Mrs Frank Dawson

Mrs Sharon Fallon

Mr Peter Frost & Family

Mr Herbert (Bill) Humphrey

Mr Paul Kind

Miss Margaret Mackintosh

Mr Peter Mortimer

Mrs Grace Pratt

And special thanks to

Mr Alan Sutton, Australia

In 1973 a Nestlé Rowntree Band historian wrote:

> *' Today, the Band is a most virile and progressive organisation with a full membership and an enthusiastic team of good instrumentalists.'*

> *'All in all, Rowntree's Band is an organisation which seeks gratification from making music of a high standard and, most of all, pleasing other people.'*

You will see, as you progress through this book, that - whilst the name of the band may have changed (on many occasions), the fortunes of the band may have varied, and the personnel 'behind the stands' has inevitably changed – these two statements could have been applied to us at any point, and could just as easily have been written today.

I have to admit that it felt a little odd, as a foreigner (from Scotland) and a woman (in a brass band!) to be asked to compile this history of our band. However, I feel proud and honoured to do so. Having read, from cover to cover, every piece of archived material I could get my hands on – the sense of history and wonderment I have at being a link in this very long chain has been overwhelming.

In excess of 1,000 individuals have 'played their parts' in making this band what it is today. Many of these are long dead and buried, but no less a vital part of our history. It is my fervent hope, as I compile this book that I can do some justice to the men and women who came before me, and pave the way for those still to come.

Yes, this book covers 100 years of our history, but make no mistake, this is just the beginning…we've only just begun…

Sharon J. Lang

INTRODUCTION

In the beginning there was chocolate,
and the chocolate was good.

And so it came to pass that the chocolate factory
desired a band and a band was formed
– the year was 1903….

But even before that…

Henry Isaac Rowntree took over the business of manufacturing cocoa and chocolate from Tuke & Co., in 1862. Tuke & Co. had been producing cocoa and chocolate since the late 18th century. Henry was later joined by his brother, Joseph, and together they set up a factory in Tanners Moat. Initially they employed a dozen men, but by 1894, the workforce had grown to 864.

In 1890, they purchased land and built the new 'Cocoa Works', factory and production was gradually transferred over to this Haxby Road site. By 1904 the number employed at the Haxby Road Factory was 2,945.

It is beyond dispute that Joseph Rowntree was a man who was extremely aware of the social problems of his time. In 1899 he published his research entitled 'The Temperance Problem and Social Reform' in which he detailed his findings on drink related problems. He was deeply interested in the human aspect of factory management and appointed one of the earliest social workers within a factory. It was he who insisted on the provision of spacious, light, clean and airy buildings, surrounded by lawns, trees and flowers (an ideal arena for the 'lunchtime concerts' which were to be given following the formation of the works brass band.

In the 16th edition 'Cocoa Works Magazine' dated June, 1903, the following remarks were placed, under the 'Notes and News' section:

'It has been suggested that the formation of a Brass Band in connection with the Works would be welcomed by many musical enthusiasts in our midst. The project will have careful consideration if it is likely to meet with sufficient support to ensure its success, and we shall be glad to have the names of those employees who are willing to join if such a band is formed, names should be sent to D.S. Crighton or F.H. Hope before the end of the month.'

Mr Anthony Lickley, conductor of The Groves Wesleyan Band, replied, as did most of the members of his band, the company agreed to purchase the band instruments (even though records showed that some of these instruments were 50 years old), and so the first Cocoa Works Band was formed.

100 Years of

Nestlé Rowntree Band

1903 - 2003

The earliest minuted General Meeting of the band took place on 7th September 1905. Below you will find the entries made at that first meeting as the band gradually formed a committee, a constitution and formalised membership, accounting and organisation.

Meeting of Band & Committee held on Thursday the 7th September 1905.

Present   Mr Crichton (in the chair)
          Mr Lee
          and all members of the Band (23 in number)

As only two of the Committee were able to be present the General Meeting was adjourned until Tuesday the 3rd October and this Meeting thrown open for complaints and suggestions.

Mr Crichton reported that the Directors had to-day granted £10 towards the Band trip to the Crystal Palace Contest.

Suggestions:-

(1) Committee to be constituted as follows:- 4 members of Band. 4 outside members to be elected by the Band, and 3 to be nominated by the Directors.

(2) Auditors to be one member of Band independent of Committee and one appointed by the Committee.

(3) Subscriptions to be one penny per week. Every member to pay up to the 1st May last. Sub. Committee to settle date by which arrears must be paid. Any member more than six weeks in arrear to be suspended at the discretion of the Committee.

(4) (a) Fines to be discontinued or
    (b) New Rule made so as to ensure members attendance at practice.

(5) Rule as to misbehaviour of Bandsmen to be made.

(6) Committee to meet about once a month.

(7) Librarian to be elected and ? have a salary.

(8) Engagements to be notified to the members about a
fortnight before if possible & to be posted up in
Band room.

(10) As to payment for Engagements:-
(a) Everyone alike
(b) Time lost first +then all alike
(c) Committee to look to attendance before paying
any money.

(11) Scale of charges to be drawn up for engagements
outside works.

(12) Band Sub-Committee to meet General Committee elected
as follows:- Cundill, Pearson, Gofton, Gunnell, +Stainsby.

(13) That re-organisation of Band be left with the Bandmaster.

The band committee quickly settled down to the business of setting
membership fees, payment for engagements and rules to govern the
conduct of members during rehearsals and beyond. As you will see
one suggestion was a rule to ensure attendance. To date the rule hasn't
been invented that can ensure members attend rehearsals. We all wish
it had.

An interesting comparison can be made here: the membership fee in
1905 was 1d per week, making the annual membership 4s 4d (or 22p
approximately in decimal currency). This year (2003) our band
membership fees for the senior band are £30.00, which is roughly 136
times more.

Also worthy of note, is the fact that the bandsmen were paid for their
attendance at engagements. The first calculation was of 'lost time'
meaning unearned wages due to attendance. Then the remainder was

equally divided between those who performed. These days, not only do individuals not get payment for performances, instead we are expected to get ourselves to and from the majority of concerts and contests as it costs the band too much money to hire a bus.

Originally, the band was made up almost exclusively from employees. These days we have only one employee left in the band (Dennis Stamp). The rest of the members come from far and wide and over recent years we've had doctors, nurses, pilots and secretaries to name but a few in our midst.

The first minuted Committee meeting took place on 15th September, 1905 and read:

Meeting held on Friday the 15th Sept'r 1905.

Present   Mr. E. Grantham (in the Chair)
- Pollard
- Randles
- Crichton
- Buckle
- Pearson
- Cundill
- Gofton
- Gunnell
- Stainsby
- A. Lickley Sen'r
- A. Lickley Jun'r
- G. H. Dook.

The Minutes of the last Meeting were read.

Proposed by Mr. Lickley   Seconded by Mr. Pollard
That we have President, Vice President & Honorary Subscribers

Proposed by Mr Crichton   Seconded by Mr Pollard
    That the committee consist of 4 members of the Band,
4 members outside members elected by the Band, and 3
nominated by the Directors.

Proposed by Mr Randles.   Seconded by Mr Cundill
    That the minimum subscription of the Hon: Subscribers
be 2/6 per annum.

Proposed by Mr Pollard   Seconded by Mr Randles
    That all engagements be charged for except in such
cases as the Committee may deem it wise to give the
services of the Band free-

Proposed by Mr Randles   Seconded by Mr Gofton
    That the minimum charge for the services of the
Band be 15/- & refreshments for any engagement in
connection with the works and £1-1-0 & refreshments
outside the works.

Proposed by Mr Randles   Seconded by Mr Pollard
    That in paying Bandsmen for engagements all
broken time, Band expenses &c. be paid first and the
Balance of all such engagements left in a Fund to

Proposed by Mr Cundill   Seconded by Mr Pollard
    That the weekly subscriptions start again as from
the 1st October - Any member being more than six
weeks in arrear to be suspended at the discretion of
the Committee.

Proposed by Mr Cundill   Seconded by Mr Pollard
    That any member of the Band out of employment
be exempt from payment of subscriptions during that
time -

Proposed by Mr Gofton   Seconded by Mr Pollard
    That this Meeting be adjourned to Friday
next the 22nd inst at 7-30 p.m.

So began the 'tweaking' of rules and constitution to find the best
balance to suit both the band and its' members. There was obviously a
great deal to sort.

Those instruments… some of which were already 50 years old, had to be overhauled. So far, a permanent bandroom had not been allocated – rehearsals were taking place in a variety of corridors and rooms around the buildings. There was nowhere, as yet to store spare instruments or anywhere to house the growing library of music.

However, essentials were being dealt with. The Librarian (without library) was allocated a 5 shillings per year salary (25p); the committee would be meeting once per month; and the name of the firm or its monogram was to be placed on the uniform caps.

At the first (proper) General Meeting on 3rd October 1905, 10 members of the band and Mr Crichton (in the Chair) were present. From this number they elected the committee to be composed as follows:

Band Members:- Messrs Slainsby, Cundill, Gunnell and Pearson

Outside Members (elected by the Band):- Messrs E. Grantham, Buckle, Pollard and Lawrence
3 to be nominated by the Directors

The following appointments were also made:
Bandmaster:-   *Mr A. Lickley (Snr)*
Assistant to:-   *Mr Vasey*
Secretaries:-   *Mr A. Lickley (Jnr) & G.H. Hook*
Librarian:-   *Mr Barker*
Auditor:-   *Mr F. Gofton*
Treasurer:-   *left for Committee to elect*

The names of those attending the next General Meeting, which was held on 10th September 1906, are listed in full and the list reads:

Mr Crichton (in the Chair);
Messrs Grantham, Barrell, Buckle, Pollard, A. Lickley (Snr), Pearson, Anderson, Diggles, Barker, E. Sutton, Richmond, G. Lickley, Gunnell, Buckle (Jnr) Cattley, Byers, Cundill, Vasey, Hawksby, F. Gofton, Lee, A. Lickley (Jnr), G. Foote

The Band Meeting (at practice) on 20th August 1907, lists the following members present:

Lickley (Snr), Leray, Howe, Vasey, Foote, Watson, Buckle, E. Sutton, T. Sellers, Harrison, Crimlis, Slainsby, Gunnell, Diggles, Richmond, Anderson, T. Buckle, G. Lickley, Barker, Pearson, Jos. Sutton, Moses, Cundill, A. Lickley (Jnr) (24)
with apologies from: Hawksby, I. Lickley & Dalton

These are the players in the photograph overleaf and it is the founder, Mr A. Lickley (Snr), who is wielding the baton.

So here we are, it's 1905, we have a band that is rehearsing twice weekly, giving local concerts and tentatively planning to venture into the world of contesting. 'But, they are playing on 50 year old instruments', I hear, 'and they don't have a bandroom, either!'. I know, I know, but as Confucius once said 'every great journey begins with a single step'.

Most 2 year olds can manage to toddle about quite securely, and so it was with the Cocoa Works Band. They ably helped to organise the 1st (highly successful) 'Horticultural Show and Brass Band Contest', which was held in the grounds of the factory. Two more of these contests were held and visited by some of the great bands of their day. But when the band itself finally took the plunge (just 4 years after being formed) it was an immediate success. The band entered the 1907 Crystal Palace Contest (albeit the Preliminary Cup Section) on 28th September and came, an extremely satisfying, second out of 19 competitors.

The band had employed a professional conductor, Mr G. Mallinson, during the latter part of 1906, to give lessons to the band at a cost of 5 shillings (25p) per time, for an initial period of 6 months. It can be assumed that he was extremely good value given that within a year the band came second at such a prestigious competition. For attending the Crystal Palace Contest with the band, Mr Mallinson was sent his expenses, 30 shillings (£1.50). Additionally, the Directors agreed to engage Mr Mallinson for a further six months.

This success would not have been possible without the help of the Directors. Having first been approached on the subject of new instruments for the band during February 1906, new instruments were indeed bought, in January 1907. The total cost of these instruments (the cost also included 'B' quality cases) was £169=4=6 (£169.22p). This generosity, enabled the purchase of a number of first class instruments namely: 4 cornets; 2 flugel horns, 2 tenor horns, 2 baritone horns, 1 euphonium; 2 tenor trombones, 3 Bb basses and 1 Eb bass (almost an entire band set of beautiful new instruments) (pictured overleaf). In the accounts of the band, dated 14th July 1904, it shows the purchase of a 'Cornet, Boosey' and the cost was £5.25 – compared with today's price of around £1,400. Such a generous donation of instruments was met with utter delight amongst the band.

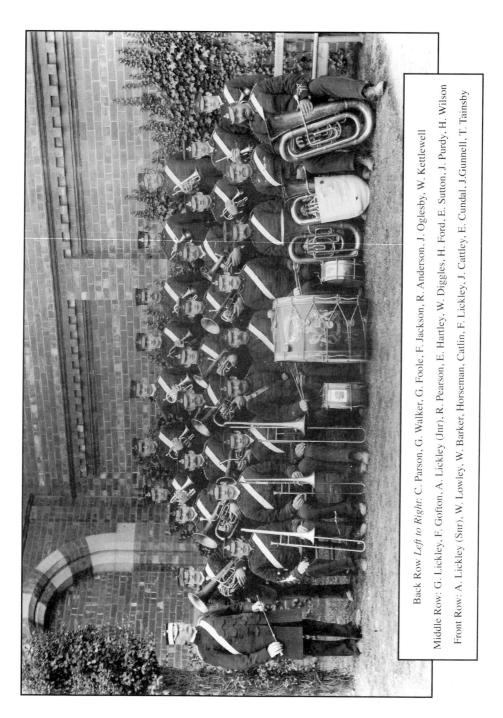

Back Row *Left to Right*: C. Parson, G. Walker, G. Foole, F. Jackson, R. Anderson, J. Oglesby, W. Kettlewell

Middle Row: G. Lickley, F. Gofton, A. Lickley (Jnr). R. Pearson, E. Hartley, W. Diggles, H. Ford, E. Sutton, J. Purdy, H. Wilson

Front Row: A. Lickley (Snr), W. Lowley, W. Barker, Horseman, Catlin, F. Lickley, J. Cattley, E. Cundal, J.Gunnell, T. Tainsby

Obtaining the new instruments allowed for the older instruments to be used in the formation of the first 'Junior Band'. On 11th January 1907, it was proposed *'that members of the Committee look out for likely lads to be trained for the Junior Band'.* . (The subscription for Junior Band Members was to be 2d per month (10p per year, ah how things change). Mr G. Lickley (son of the conductor) was appointed to train the juniors. The 'Cocoa Works Magazine' for February 1907, contains the following comment:

> *'As there are now some instruments at liberty, the (band) Committee require a number of smart youths to form a Junior Band, and with this object in view they are commencing a class to teach anyone desirous of becoming members.'*

Scale and exercise books were bought for use by the Learners during April 1907, so it seems that there had been a reasonable response to the notice in the CWM. In fact, Mr G. Lickley reported to the Committee on 17th April 1907, that 6 Juniors were attending practice. Further notices were posted from time to time to encourage more youngsters to join the Juniors.

These Junior members were invited to join the band for the trip to the Crystal Palace Contest, in London, provided that they paid for the actual costs of including them.

Even in the midst of this success, the age old problem of attendance was rearing its head again and again. February 1908, records show that the average attendance was 19.5. I very much doubt if we could better that in our modern band.

As ever, in a brass band, things don't always run smoothly. The minutes of the band give us a marvellous insight into the social times, as well as the everyday running of the band. It was fascinating to read in the minutes, dated 13th March 1906, that *'Mr Lowley attended the meeting and fully explained his views as to being allowed to play with the Artillery Volunteer's and also with this Band'*. It is reported *'that our Rules distinctly state no member can belong to any other Brass Band. Mr Lowley be given a week from today to decide with which Band he will play'*. The saga continued on 10th April 1906 when the minutes read: *'Lowley's letter demanding a written guarantee of work was read'* when it was proposed and seconded *'that his name be struck off the register as a member of the band.'* Unsurprisingly Mr Lowley is not mentioned in the minutes again.

The rules and regulations, which are very clear read:

ROWNTREE'S BRASS BAND.

RULES AND REGULATIONS.

1. The Band shall be called "ROWNTREE'S BRASS BAND."

2. No member of the Band shall have any ownership in any of the Band property. Any member leaving the Band shall return all property belonging to the Band in such condition as shall satisfy the Committee. If the property be damaged, he shall make good.

3. A Management Committee of 11 shall be elected annually as follows:— members of Band, 4 outside members elected by Band, and 3 nominated by Director, members to form a quorum). The Bandmaster and Secretaries shall be ex-officio members of the Committee.

4. The Band shall meet at least twice a week for practice, and the Secretary shall book all present. The list of attendances shall be submitted to the Monthly Meeting of the Committee.

5. The Bandmaster, or in his absence, the selected Leader, shall have complete control of the Band. Any case of misbehaviour on the part of a Bandsman shall be reported to the Committee and dealt with by them.

6. Subscriptions shall be 1d. per week, and any member more than four weeks in arrears shall be suspended at the discretion of the Committee. Any member out of work shall be exempt from payment of subscription during that time.

7. All engagements shall be charged for, except in such cases as the Committee may deem it advisable to give the services of Band free.

8. After payment of broken time, 20% of all engagement receipts shall be put into the Band fund, and the remaining 80% shall be shared out at the end of the year in proportion to each member's actual attendance at practices and engagements. Any Bandsman not attending practices or engagements through sickness, shall be paid for the same on giving written notice thereof to the Secretaries. No Bandsman will be accepted as a Member of the Band until approved by the Committee.

9. Any Bandsman not making 2/3rds of possible attendances shall not be considered a Member of the Band, and 2/3rds of possible attendances must be put in before members are entitled to any benefits.

10. All Instruments, except the Bass Drum, must be taken home by Members.

11. No member shall play in any other Band without special permission from the Committee.

12. The Committee shall meet at least once a month.

13. All moneys must be handed to the Treasurer monthly, and all accounts be paid by him.

14. All orders must be passed through the official order book kept by the Secretary, and signed by the Chairman.

15. The Band accounts shall be audited once a year, the Auditors to be one Member of Band independent of Committee, and one elected by Committee.

I,_____ of_____

have read the above rules, and agree to abide by them, and also by the decision of the Committee in any matters concerning my connection with the Band.

Signed _____

Witness *Geo H. Fook*

Date 4th *February* 1907

The cost of printing these rules was recorded in May 1907 as 7/6 or 37p. Amendments were made to these rules during the Committee meeting on 11th January 1907:

The draft rules were read and amended and ordered to be brought before the General Meeting on Friday next for approval, with the following additions:-

(1) *That each member put in two thirds of possible attendances at practices and engagements before becoming entitled to any benefits.*

(2) *That after payment of broken time 20% of all engagements be paid into the Band fund, the remaining 80% being shared out at the end of the year in proportion to each member's actual attendances, it being left with the Bandsmen to decide whether they receive cash or use it for a trip. In the latter event, any member not being entitled to a sufficient sum to pay his proportion of expenses to make up the difference, and any member being entitled to more than his share of the cost, to have the surplus paid over to him.*

(3) *Any Bandsman not attending practices or engagements through sickness be paid for same on giving written notice thereof to the Secretaries.*

(4) *That no Bandsman be accepted as a member of the band until approved by the Committee.*

CHAPTER 2

The Cocoa Works Band rapidly made an impact on the lives of the other workers and on York residents generally.

Over the first 10 years, the band established a number of regular engagements, from the first public concert at the Hospital Garden Party in September 1903, to the numerous garden parties for the workers in the grounds of the factory.

The members of the band, with the assistance of the Directors and the Committee of the Horticultural Club, organised a brass band contest each July between 1905 and 1908 (inc.). Some of the very best bands of that era took part in these contests. The winners in 1905 were – Wyke Temperance; 1906 – Wingate Temperance; 1907 – Crosfields Soap Works and at the final contest in 1908 – Black Dyke (probably the most famous brass band in the world).

These early years saw the band compete successfully at a number of contests, e.g. Crystal Palace, Ilkley, Malton and Normanton to name but a few. Due to this success, it was decided to change the name from the Cocoa Works Band to Rowntree's Cocoa Works Prize Band (1908). Throughout all of this time the Company was unfailing in its support of the band. Mr Oscar Rowntree was the Vice-President and he and Mr Arnold Rowntree frequently sent letters of congratulations to the band on their many successes. The Company always gave the best consideration to the needs of the band with regard to uniforms, instruments and the costs of hiring a professional conductor.

Sadly, their first professional conductor, Mr H. Mallinson died in December 1910. He was described posthumously as a painstaking and successful teacher. Due to his illness the band was taken to the 1910 Crystal Palace Contest by Mr W. Halstead . Mr Halstead also took Black Dyke Juniors to the same contest, in the same section. He triumphed with a remarkable 1st and 2nd place with the bands. Black Dyke Juniors got 1st place and Rowntree's got 2nd .

As ever attendance at band practices was a problem. The available players were not always suited to the position they held and had to be moved around, and in the case of Mr Harrison, late of the flugel horn, he was requested to join the Juniors until he became more proficient!

On the death of Mr Mallinson, Mr Halstead was invited to be the band's professional conductor. Mr Halstead had been auditioned during August 1910, as well as a Mr Ambler and Mr Moore. The minutes state that if none of the above were suitable a Mr Holdsworth would be given a trial.

In the event Mr Halstead was found to be eminently suited for the position. However Mr Halstead required payment for his professional tuition of an additional £8:9:0 (£8.45) per year. As the band was not able to meet this cost it was agreed to approach the Directors with a view to their allowing the extra money for Mr Halstead's services. I assume that the company acquiesced as Mr Halstead did indeed take the band to a number of contests and gave tuition on a regular basis. Mr Halstead also assisted in the recruitment of players. On one occasion he wrote to the Committee to suggest a cornet player, Mr Tideswell, whom the Committee invited to band rehearsals on trial before finally offering a position to him on the Solo Cornet line.

The minutes of November 1911 lists the band personnel at that time to be:

Soprano Cornet	*L. Fawcett*
Solo Cornets	*Howe, Tideswell, Buckle*
Repiano	*H. Wreghitt, J. Lee*
2nd Cornet	*Sellers*
3rd Cornet	*C. Ward, A. Sutton*
Bb Basses	*Crimlis, Barker & Richmond*
Eb Basses	*Diggles & Cundill*
G Trombone	*G. Calvert*
2nd Trombone	*Smith & T. Ward*
Solo Trombone	*I. Buckle*
Euphonium	
Baritones	*W. Facett, King & Watson*
Tenors	*Foote & E. Sutton*

Mr Watson was causing some concern at this time and he had been offered a tenor position which he had refused. It was decided that Mr Lee (Chairman) and Mr A Lickley (Jnr) (Secretary) should see Mr Watson and *'if he is unable to reconsider his decision then his resignation be accepted'*. I can't find any evidence of his resignation being offered prior to this but the Committee meant business. The situation was taken very seriously. Happily an amicable solution was found soon after when Mr King agreed to go onto tenor and Mr Watson was permitted to retain his position on 2nd baritone. Whew! The vacant euphonium position was finally filled by Mr Ainsworth in January 1912 and at the same time Mr Crimlis was accepted onto the new position of BBb Bass.

Interestingly there is no mention of the drummers on any of the 'band personnel' lists. There were in fact at least 2 drummers, a side drum player and a bass drum player. One of these, Mr Barnes (side drummer) was asked in September 1912 to return his instrument. No explanation is given within the minutes for this, we could assume that poor attendance, or perhaps illness had caused this but in reality we just don't know.

In November 1911 at the Annual General Meeting, Mr A. Lickley (Snr) resigned his post as Bandmaster. Mr Lickley, as we know, had been fundamental to the formation of the band in 1903 and it was with the deepest regrets that the band accepted his decision. His brother Mr G. Lickley was duly appointed Bandmaster. He had been Deputy Bandmaster for many years, had been the Bandmaster for the Juniors since 1907 and was deemed to be sufficiently experienced for the job.

During this time many of the committee meetings and Annual General Meetings were rounded off with a Whist Drive. Prizes were given to the top 3 players. The prizes varied from a pipe to a match box and there was even a booby prize which was regularly won by the same player. In the interests of fairness, and to save embarrassment to his family, I'm not going to name him.

There was great sadness expressed in April 1912 at the death of Mr Joe Gunnell (Bass player). He is reported as having been *'an interesting old soldier who was Lord Robert's trumpeter'*.

The whist drives continued as did the competing in contests.

There is a gap in the band minutes between November 1912 and November 1913. We do however know from various sources that the band continued to be both active and successful. The band took part in the Armley Contest in June 1913 and got 3rd place in the Keighley March Contest the following June. They did numerous concerts in the Museum Gardens and Works Garden Parties. There was a thoroughly enjoyable afternoon and evening concert given at the height of the summer for York Corporation.

The band was given a brand new set of uniforms and wore them for the official opening of the Dining Block in June 1912. On the page opposite is the receipt for the purchase of these uniforms.

Isn't it amazing that a full set of bandsmen's tunics, trousers and caps plus the band conductor's uniform came to a total of £48.20. We have only recently renewed some of our band jackets (only jackets mind you) and each jacket costs approximately £160.00.

September saw the band compete once more in the Crystal Palace Contest. There was to be no prize this year sadly (they had won 5 prizes out of the previous 6 years). The contest places had been drawn and the band were drawn 4th in order of play. The test piece for the Junior Section was 'Classic Gems', an old favourite, and the band were well prepared for the occasion. The bands which had been drawn 1st, 2nd and 3rd were unable to turn out a full band and were therefore unable to take part in the competition. As any bandsman will tell you this caused complete uproar and forced the band to hasten their performance which no doubt affected their playing.

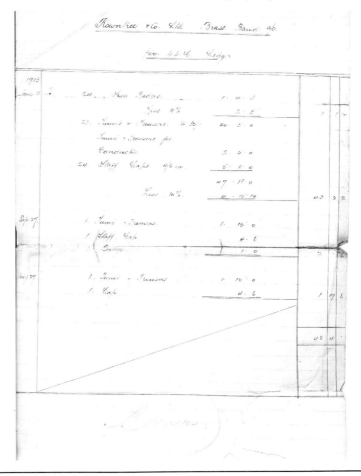

After breakfast at the hotel Mr A. Lickley (Jnr) presented (on behalf of the members of the band) a silver watch and guard to Mr H. Tideswell. Mr Tideswell was leaving the band and emigrating to America. The committee subsequently agreed to *'engage a new cornet player if it is possible to get him work'.* If only talent could ensure employment these days!

ROWNTREE'S COCOA WORKS PRIZE BAND.

RULES and REGULATIONS.

1. The Band shall be called "Rowntree's Cocoa Works Prize Band".

2. No Member shall have any ownership in any of the Band property Any Member leaving the Band shall return all property belong--ing to the Band in such condition as shall satisfy the Committee. If the property be damaged he shall make it good.

3. A Management Committee shall be elected annually as follows:-
    An equal number of Members of the Band and outside Members elected by the Band (such number to be decided at the annual Meeting) and 3 nominated by the Directors (5 Members to form a quorum). The Bandmasters and Secretaries shall be ex-officio members of the Committee.

4. The Band shall meet at least twice a week for practice and the Secretary shall book all present. The list of attendances shall be submitted to the Monthly Meeting of the Committee. Any member not present at practices or engagements within half an hour of the recognised time of starting without a reasona -able excuse shall only receive half attendance mark.

5. The Bandmaster or in his absence the selected Leader shall have complete control of the Band. Any case of misbehaviour on the part of a Bandsman shall be reported to the Committee and be dealt with by them.

6. Subscriptions shall be at the rate of One penny per week and must be paid by the 30th September in each year.

7. All engagements shall be charged for except in such cases as the Committee may deem it advisable to give the serives of the Band Free.

8. After payment of broken time and other expenses all engagement receipts shall be put into the Band Fund and after retaining a small balance to be fixed by the Committee the remainder shall be shared out at the end of the year in proportion to each members actual attendance at practices and engagements. Any Bandsman not attending practices or engagements through sickness shall be paid for the same on giving written notice thereof to the Secretaries.

9. No Bandsman will be accepted as a member of the Band until approved by the Committee.

10. All instruments except the Bass Drum must be taken home by members except under special circumstances.

11. No Member shall play in any York Brass Band without special permission from the Committee. ~~and this Band shall have the first call on its members.~~

12. All items of expenditure over 5/- must be sanctioned by the Committee.

13. The Band Accounts shall be audited once a year the Auditors to be one Member of the Band independent of Committee and one elected by the Committee.

14. When on parade the Bandmaster shall have power (according to his discretion) to order players to assist in carrying the Bass instrucments.

It was not until the very end of 1913 that the original Rules and Regulations were updated as follows:

The only significant change was to the 2/3rds attendance rule. This was changed to reflect that members would be paid in proportion to their attendance at both rehearsals and concerts. A small amendment to Rule 11 was made at the meeting to agree these changes and it was stated that *'on short notice the Bandmaster should be empowered to give permission'*.

January 1914 saw the band attempt a slightly new venture. It was agreed to hold an 'open' Whist Drive. Mr Buckle was to be entrusted with the catering arrangements – cost 6d (2p) per head with admission being 1 shilling (5p). There would be 1st, 2nd and 3rd prizes for both ladies and gentlemen. The evening was a great success making the band a profit of £2:0:5. The committee planned to hold further open whist drives and continued to hold the monthly drive after committee meetings. A suggestion to hold an open-air whist drive during the summer was being considered.

In February 1914 the band was approached to accompany dancing at the York Gala. Attendances at rehearsals were consistently above 19 (on average). Requests for the band to perform at local shows and garden parties were increasing. Many applications were being received from players wishing to join the band. Some applications were put on hold until such time as the applicants were able to secure employment, the band having been unsuccessful in finding employment on their behalf.

One such application was from a Mr Neale. It was proposed and seconded that he be accepted on trial for a month (this was normal practice) and that it be left to the conductor to decide whether he should be accepted. Just a week later the minutes read *'Neales cornet had been obtained as he had turned out to be a deserter'*.

In the midst of all this, there must have been seeds of doubt germinating, the committee decided not to enter the Belle Vue (Manchester) Contest (which was subsequently cancelled). In fact as early as April 1914, it was recorded that *'the question of attending any contest be left over for the present'*.

Still Garden Parties went ahead, dates were agreed for June, July and August. A selection of Dance Music was obtained and the bandmaster was empowered to see about a Music Cupboard.

The band, you may remember, was still without a proper practice room. This issue had cropped up time and again but as yet was unresolved.   April 1914 saw the band arranging to have the necessary lights fixed in place in order to practice OUTSIDE! It was May, however before the lights were ready.

All of this was overshadowed in the most dramatic way. War was declared on 4th August 1914.

So, what to do now!

Well, obviously no further contesting would be done. The band trip to Crystal Palace was cancelled. The August Garden Party, arranged for the 12th, was postponed and a notice to this effect was placed in the Evening Press.

Not all players appreciated the trip being cancelled and Mr Barker applied to the committee for permission to play with the City Band at the Crystal Palace. He also wished to play with them at a concert in aid of the Local Fund. Permission was not granted as it was thought it would be detrimental to our own band. Subsequently Mr Barker submitted his resignation which was accepted and he was thanked for his past services.

The band needed to reorganise, not just as a result of Mr Barker leaving, but due to the number of players coming and going at this time. On 8th September 1914 the arrangement was:

Soprano	*Wreghitt*
Solo Cornets	*A. Howe, Fawcett, H. Buckle*
Repiano	*Vasey & Lee*
Second Cornets	*Sellers, Smallwood & Howe*
Third Cornets	*Buckle & Woodcock*
Basses	*Cundill , G. Buckle, Ward & Jackson*
G Trombone	*Richmond*
2nd Trombone	*Calvert*
Solo Trombone	*I Buckle*
Euphonium	*Hainsworth*
Solo Baritone	*Bell*
2nd Baritone	*Moses*
Horns	*Sutton (2nd), King (1st), Foote (Solo)*

(Still no mention of the drummers!!)

The band resolved to offer its services through the papers to give concerts for free provided that the necessary hall and lighting was also provided free. All the proceeds were to be given to the Local Fund. Additionally, the band offered their services in aid of the Local Relief Fund and they wrote to the Lord Mayor to offer their assistance in whichever way was deemed useful.

At this time several members were giving assistance to other bands (not always with the committee's approval) and amendments to Rule 11 were being considered. Also subscriptions were to be excused. The proposed new music was being left over for the time being. Twenty-eight men attended the final AGM, 9th December 1914 and an *'enjoyable Whist Drive was afterwards held'*.

CHAPTER 3

There continued to be rehearsals twice per week for anyone who could attend. Many did so on an irregular basis right through to the end of the Great War. By February 1919 there was deemed to be sufficient members back in circulation to formally re-establish the band.

I find it remarkable, that even when things were as tentative as this, the committee would not bend on Rule 11 (allowing players to assist other groups) as you will see from the final note of these minutes.

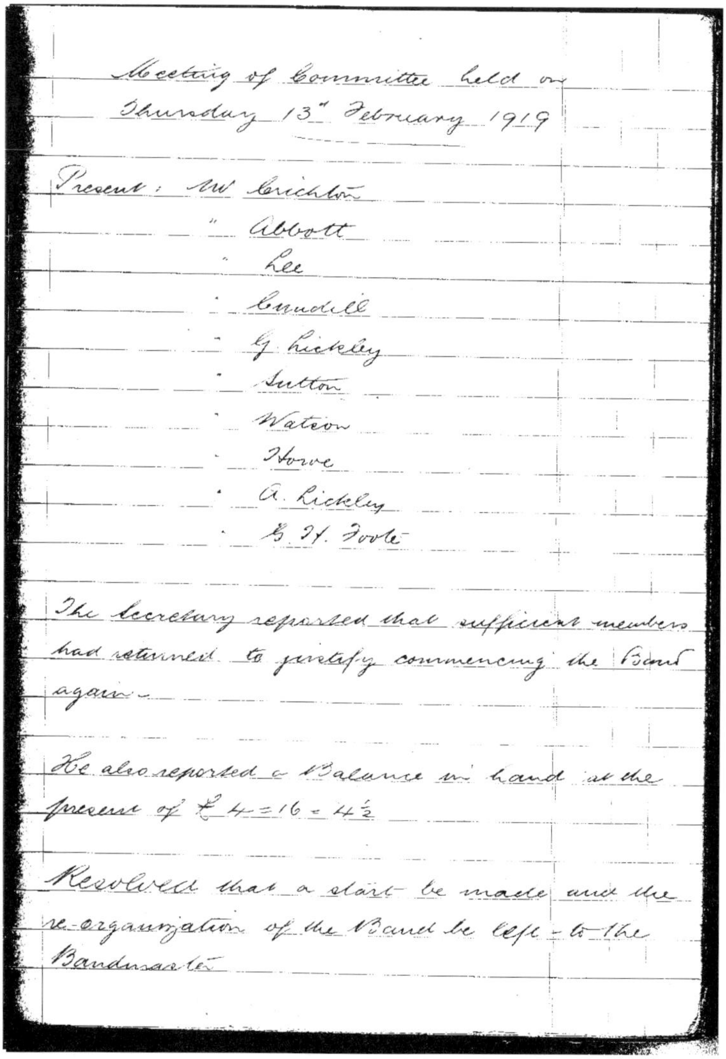

Meeting of Committee held on
Thursday 13ᵗʰ February 1919

Present: Mr Crichton
  " Abbott
  " Lee
  " Caudell
  " G. Rickley
  " Sutton
  " Watson
  " Howe
  " A. Rickley
  " B. H. Foote

The Secretary reported that sufficient members had returned to justify commencing the Band again.

He also reported a Balance in hand at the present of £4=16=4½

Resolved that a start be made and the re-organization of the Band be left to the Bandmaster

Resolved that Medd (Rive Office) be given a trial as a Playing Member

Resolved that Mr Crichton be approached to see if pressure could be brought to bear to get Richmond J. Sellers & E. Barker out of the Army.

Resolved that Practices be held on Tuesdays and Thursdays from 7-30 to 9-30.

The question of Calvert playing with the Comrades Band was mentioned when it was decided that as our Rules prohibited members belonging to 2 Bands he would have to decide which he would prefer.

May 5th
H Cundill
Chairman

Interestingly, the band asked Mr Crichton to see if *'pressure could be brought to bear to get Richmond, J. Sellers and E. Barker out of the Army'*. A fantastic insight into how a bandsman's mind works.

Practises in the meantime would continue to be held on Tuesday and Thursday evenings between 7.30 and 9.30.

By May 1919 the band numbers had risen to 26, a full compliment. Mr L. Fawcett was proposed as the band's Solo Cornet player having been the Soprano player in 1911 and subsequently a Solo Cornet player before the war. All were quite willing to allow Mr A Lickley (Jnr), Bandmaster to decide on the best arrangement of the other personnel around the stands. New music was being bought and paid engagements were once again on the band calendar.

Once again the Band Rules were debated and largely reinstated without notable changed excepting Rule 2 where 'wilful damage' was to replace 'damage and Rule 12, where the amount of expenditure requiring Committee approval was raised from 5/- (shillings)(25p) to 10/- (50p).

The General Meeting of 1919 also saw the bandsmen requesting that business discussed at Committee should be brought before the band at the practise following the meeting. Hitherto discussions at committee were treated as confidential and leaks of information were frowned upon.

Attendance at rehearsals had stabilised, once again averaging 19 (I really wish we could match this).

However the Band Cupboard had been broken into during the war and a Soprano Cornet and a Bb Cornet had been stolen. Once again the Directors were to be approached regarding the provision of a permanent Band Room. December 1920 saw the band being offered the use of the kitchen in the corridor for rehearsals. It would be 1923 before a permanent Band Room was actually provided.

By 1920 the band was once again preparing to contest. There is a driving force within most bandsmen to pit their skills and abilities against other like-minded individuals. It is almost impossible to explain this. There is a deep-seated need to be the best at what you do and to prove it beyond question to your peers. The 2003 band is no different in this respect. We are constantly challenging ourselves to improve and compete with and against the best bands in the country. Success at Championship level is rare, but sweet when it does come.

Mr Halstead was re-employed as the band's Professional Conductor during 1920 and tasked with making sufficient progress with the players so that they would once again be able to take part in the contest arena. It had been some time since the band had taken part in a contest The prizes had gone up and the band formation was changing from the traditional square form to the new, modern, U form. I've illustrated on the page opposite how brass bands originally had formed up and it makes an interesting comparison with how they are now traditionally arranged.

Our band had happily anticipated the formation changes but others were less prepared and refused to play in the new shape at the 1922 and 1923 Crystal Palace Contests. Rowntree's Brass Band took fourth place in the 1923 contest.

This was the standard layout of a Brass Band, for entertaining as well as contesting, bearing in mind the players were all standing up. The smaller ones had to stand on boxes to be able to see the conductor and the music:

1. Conductor (facing 3.)
2. Solo Cornets and behind them back row cornets
3. Baritones, Horns and Soprano Cornet
4. Euphonium and Trombones
5. Basses

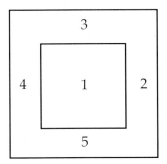

Following the changes over 1922/1923 the now familiar and traditional seated arrangement is:

1. Conductor
2. Solo Cornets, with Soprano and Back Row Cornets behind
3. Baritones and Euphoniums with Trombones behind
4. Flugel and Tenor Horns with Basses behind

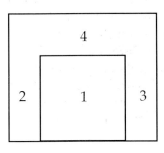

We also have 2 or 3 percussionists (drummers) now who are placed to either side of the basses, depending on the space available.

As early as March, 1920, the band's attendance had risen to an average of 20 players per rehearsal. This was a fantastic endorsement to the members. The perennial problem of rehearsals starting on time was still an issue – as it is today.

The band swung into action with barely a look back. Fundraising concerts, garden parties, contests and whist drives were all back on the agenda. New uniforms were requested, old instruments were being sold and new ones ordered. The memory of the war era was being put firmly behind the band and the future once again was looking very bright. The band played for the opening of Huntington Memorial Hall during the August Bank Holiday (1920) and charged £17:5:0 for the engagement.

Funds as ever were low and so the Company was asked if the band could give lunchtime concerts in the Rose Gardens to increase funds. This was agreed to. A regular garden party at the football grounds, Bootham Crescent, was often suggested. The directors at Bootham Park however did not agree to this as a fundraising plan for the band and despite frequent requests this never quite came off. Even the use of the Earswick football ground was difficult as during May and August a garden party might interfere with the hay crop. However, during the summer this field was handed over to the Girls Rounders Club. It was agreed that the band could use it each Wednesday, if a contribution to the upkeep expenses, about £12 for the season, was made. So garden parties were arranged and the band played for dances and also organised a couple of children's races during the intervals.

December 1920 saw an age old dilemma rear its head. Two players competing for the same position. In brief, Mr Milligan had been the band's G Trombone player until circumstances caused him to resign his position reluctantly. A replacement was found in Mr Brown who due to wounds in his back was reluctant to move to another instrument. Fortunately Mr Milligan's situation altered enabling him to retain his membership. In fact Mr Milligan had recommended Mr Brown as his replacement. The committee allowed Mr Milligan back to his position, lost Mr Brown in the process and when Mr Milligan subsequently moved to Hull (Feb. 1921) the band was temporarily without a G Trombonist.

There was a slight relaxation of Rule 11 during 1921, when Mr Jowsey tendered his resignation. The committee had no desire to lose this valuable player and Mr Buckle suggested that "there would be no objection to members playing with other bands provided that whilst doing so, they do not interfere with the progress of this band". What a breakthrough.

The band was having no success during this period attracting likely juniors to train up to be senior members and due to the unemployment in York at the time, players such as Mr Cousins from York, who wanted to join, had to be turned down as there was no hope of employment within the factory so as to enable membership.

CHAPTER 4

The Sutton Family

From the first rehearsal in 1903 until 1992 there was a member of the Sutton family in the band. There were many years in fact when there were 3 of them and occasionally even more:

This photograph shows E.E. Sutton (centre) who was one of the founding members of the band, flanked by his sons E. Sutton (Ted)(right) and J. Sutton (Johnny)(left) – *photograph by kind permission of Johnny's son Alan.*

Besides having his Grandfather, Uncle (Ted, Jnr) and Father, in the band Alan Sutton also had his two uncles (his mother's brothers) and he and his brother were also members. With such a history it is only fair that Alan and his family should be allowed to tell their own story with just a little clarification from the archives where necessary:

E E Sutton (Grandad)

Ted (Snr) was born in Hull in 1882 and lived at Welton. It was said in the family that Grandad or part of his family had traced the family tree as far back as Ethelred the Great.

I could see where Dad (Johnny) got his professionalism from as Grandad used to give me heaps. Whilst I was in the band he played tenor horn and was always at band practise. Away from the band I called on Grandad and Grandma every weekend. The last time I saw Grandad was at Dads before he moved to Newcastle to live with my Auntie Doris.

For most of his time with the band Mr Sutton was an active and vocal member of the committee. He was an extremely hardworking player as well and was content to play almost any instrument provided the needs of the band were met. He mostly played on the tenor horn but was known to pick up the euphonium, baritone or even cornet when needed. For a long time he was a committee member and the band Registrar, the member who recorded attendance and collected subscriptions.

E A Sutton (Uncle Ted)

I came into contact with Uncle Ted and family on a regular basis. I would call round there to watch TV. He had been in the Navy during the war; I think he was in the engine room as he had a lot of engineering knowledge.

Ted (Jnr) worked in the big power plant at the factory and later transferred to the sub station alongside the railway line. He was the same as Dad when it came to music, I remember when he had his teeth out he changed from cornet to euphonium, he would spend every spare minute he had practicing. He would even go to the band room in his lunch hour. All the practice paid off, I remember that when I joined the band he had a beautiful tone. I last saw Uncle Ted in 1987 at my mother's funeral. He was still visiting the band room in those days.

During the distribution of monies paid by the Farmers Association in April 1930, it was proposed by L. Fawcett and seconded by H. Wreghitt that Ted be given a donation of £1, in view of him being unemployed – this was agreed to. In January 1931 the same proposal was made and accepted – we are ever grateful for these decisions as it allowed Ted to continue with the band despite his unemployment and he remained a willing, active member until his death in 1992. Ted was band Librarian for the last 40 years of his life and was still a playing member until his final illness.

L. Fawcett (Uncle Len)

I did not see Uncle Len in the band. I was very young when he died. As a child I remember I used to visit his house, he was very good at making models and I was fascinated by this hobby. He was my mother's brother and one of five brothers.

Len was an active committee member for many years, he was also assistant bandmaster during the 1930's. He was the instigator of many band 'raffles' and showed great initiative and willingness in aiding the bands financial position with these.

E Fawcett (Uncle Ted)

Uncle Ted used to live round the corner from us. After his wife died my mum used to do his cleaning and washing on a Monday. I played alongside him in the trombone section where he played G trombone. Once again, he died when I was a teenager.

The thing I recall most was that in those days the bandsmen took their music very seriously and were very professional. When I watch 'Brassed Off' I get a few tears in my eyes as the conductor reminds me of my dad - nothing stops him until he has it right.

The Musical Career of Johnny Sutton
by Alan Sutton.

(Johnny Sutton was accepted as a full member of the band on 15th November 1921 he served on the committee from 1930 and was an active vocal committee man.)

Johnny Sutton (1906 – 1973)

I am only able to put some approximate dates to some of the events that follow. My dad, Johnny was introduced to music by his father, E.E. Sutton, who was a founder member of the Cocoa Works Band. There is a photograph, at the start of this chapter, which was taken in 1922. It shows my dad with his brother Ted and their father in it He would have been around 16 years of age at this time.

As a young person he was interested in keeping fit and used to spend time at the works gym. It was this that led to him having an accident that was to affect the way he played his instrument. He would run up the backyard and launch himself into the air so that he landed on the window ledge. On one such occasion he failed to pull his right arm down quick enough and it went through the window severing an artery and the tendon that controls the middle finger.

I don't want to be too gory but the story goes that the blood spurted over a 6ft wall and reached the neighbour's back door. A tourniquet was applied and towels wrapped round the wound and he walked to the York County Hospital for treatment. The artery was repaired, but not with microsurgery which did not exist at this time. The severed tendon was tied to the next finger tendon hence his 2nd and 3rd fingers went up and down together. The players amongst you will appreciate that this makes playing a valve instrument very difficult. However anyone who knew Dad would know that he loved his music so much that this was not going to stop him playing. With great determination he learned to play his cornet using the left hand for the valves.

During the Second World War he turned his attention to dance bands. He firstly formed the Modernaires and they played at venues like the Milton Rooms in Malton, the Coop Hall Railway

Street (where they went on to be the resident band) and at the De Grey Rooms. In the mid fifties the personnel of the dance band changed and it was renamed 'Johnny Sutton and his Music'. The members of this band came from a big band that Dad had put together with Barry Prendergast (John Barry) to play his arrangements. John Barry was just one of the many people who came to Dad for help and experience.

Dad worked at the factory during the day, and so he was classed as a semi – professional musician. He worked in block packing, which entailed packing 1cwt blocks of chocolate for transportation. In 1960 he was found to have angina and needed time off work to convalesce. His doctor suggested that he should stop playing his trumpet. His reply was that he would rather die earlier being happy than last a few more years and be miserable. Rowntree's sent him to Scarborough to their convalescent home for 2 weeks. Naturally, he took his trumpet with him. However, the matron would not let him practise (it disturbed the other patients). I took the car to him for his second week there and he would get up very early in the morning and go up Oliver's Mount to practise. His last piece each morning would be 'Come to the Cook House'. He played this to let matron know he was coming down for breakfast.

Dad thought he was practicing in a secluded spot and didn't realise the whole of Scarborough was listening to him. It caused quite a stir as people were trying to find out where the music was coming from. The tale made the morning national papers with the headline "The Phantom Trumpeter". Questions were asked of the professional musicians working in Scarborough for the summer season. They all agreed that it couldn't be a professional as it was too early in the morning. Dad's pianist Geoff Knaggs finally solved the mystery. Geoff saw the article, put two and two together and gave Dad's secret away to the Yorkshire Evening Press.

Eventually Dad returned to work in the conch room where he would check the viscosity of the chocolate while it was being mixed. After a time, though, his heart got the better of him and he was put on permanent sick leave.

The band finished at the De Grey rooms in 1963 and went from there to do a winter season at Bridlington Spa Ballroom. When that ended there wasn't work for big bands so Dad didn't go out on jobs, instead he helped young people form bands and gave them free tuition. "He never gives up" was the comment one band leader made after enquiring where Dad was and I told him he was at the 'Winning Post' with a group of young musicians.

Dad was diagnosed with cancer in February 1973 and died late 1973.

After I left for Australia, in 1968 Dad returned to the Cocoa Works Band and did some conducting. He was well known in the town for his attention to detail, I am sure the band welcomed this. Dad restarted a junior band, as this was one of his skills - he gave great encouragement to young musicians

The headmaster of a private school at Mill Mount rang Dad and said they were going to form a band. He wanted Dad to go and give advice as to what instruments they might need to buy. Once they had the instruments the headmaster rang again and told Dad 'we have the instruments, but what do we do now?' Dad in his usual way went along, started and taught the band for nothing, up to the day he died.

Apparently when he got too ill to drive the school would send a taxi for him and off he would go, dragging his oxygen bottle along behind him. The cutting overfeaf from the York Evening Press says it all, it's a pity people have to die before it is said.

YORK DANCE BAND LEADER DIES AT 67

DANCE BAND leader Johnny Sutton, whose music was enjoyed by thousands of post-war dancers at York's De Grey Roms, died in hospital in York, last night.

Johnny, who was 67 and one of York's best-known musicians, had been ill for some months. He leaves a widow and two sons. One of them—Alan—who used to play drums with his father's band, is in Australia.

A musician from his very early days, Johnny—who played trumpet and cornet—came from a musical family.

His father was a founder-member of the Rowntree Cocoa Works Band—which Johnny himself joined and later conducted.

Throughout his life, Johnny, whose home was at 24 Southolme Drive, Shipton Road, York, encouraged young people to take an interest in music, and latterly he ran the very successful junior band of Rowntree Mackintosh.

John Barry, now one of the world's top film music writers, was helped in his early musical career in York by Johnny Sutton.

Associated with The Modernaires, who for several years were the acknowledged leading dance band in the York area, Johnny Sutton later formed his own Johnny Sutton Band, which became synonymous with dancing at York's De Grey Rooms in the 1950s.

The band also took part in a number of band contests.

Ted Pratt, now a music teacher, who played in the trumpet section of the Johnny Sutton Band for several years, said today: "There are a lot of musicians in York who have cause to be grateful to Johnny Sutton for the help he gave them, and the way he encouraged them to a high standard of musicianship."

CHAPTER 5

Back to the happenings in the bandroom and beyond

1922 saw the band of St Hilda's Colliery on tour. They wanted the Cocoa Works Band to sort out a venue for them in York and to guarantee a fee of £50. Unsurprisingly our band declined to help and passed the request onto York Corporation.

The pattern for concerts and contests was to continue relatively smoothly for the next 17 years until the events of the 2nd World War. Throughout this period the band successfully raised funds, held garden parties and competed at numerous contests.

Sadly during 1927 the band's long time bandmaster, Mr G. Lickley passed away. Mr G. Lickley was a highly regarded bandsman, teacher and conductor, having being the solo euphonium player for many years before becoming bandmaster. All admired his patience and musicianship and he was sadly missed. The band attended his funeral service and marched to York Cemetery afterwards. He was son of the original bandmaster Mr A. Lickley who continued his connection with the band in the position of Vice-Chairman. During G. Lickley's long illness Mr Hainsworth who retained the position for a further 5 years took on the conducting.

1928 was another sad year, Mr Halstead long time professional conductor died. During this year he had helped the band gain 1st Prize (March) at the Ripley Castle Band Contest and 2nd Prize (Selection) at the same contest. The band under his baton were placed 3rd at the Knaresbrough Contest and also took part in the Crystal Palace Contest. Prior to his death the band presented him with a gold mounted umbrella which had cost £3.25. He was considered to be a musician of outstanding ability, a great teacher and a gentleman.

Mrs Halstead wrote to the band in 1930 enclosing a list of pieces of music that belonged to her late husband. The band was invited to select the pieces they would like to have. Various pieces were chosen which Mrs Halstead donated to the Band who accepted them with gratitude.

The death of Mr Halstead left the position of professional conductor vacant. During the committee meeting held in March 1929 it was reported that the band had received letters from several people asking to be considered for the post. In the end the band wrote to 8 conductors to ask for their 'terms'. Several of these gentlemen ruled themselves out by being too expensive or unavailable however a Mr H.

Lambeth and Mr J.B. Wright were invited to take a rehearsal each during April. After a ballot of the members Mr Wright was selected as the new professional conductor. Mr Wright lead the band to a 2nd Place (March) in the Driffield Contest during June of that year and also took them to the Crystal Palace Contest.

Around this time the British Bandsman published a statement that declared that a Mr G. Walker had been appointed as conductor of the band. Mr Walker did indeed have a long and distinguished association with the band and served as Auditor in addition to being an active member of the committee. However he was not, at this time, the bandmaster. The Committee agreed that the secretary, Mr A. Lickley, should write to the magazine and contradict this statement. Incidentally, the band had been entered for the Pudsey, Brotheron and Manchester Contests during 1930 and withdrew from all of them owing to Mr Walker's illness!! Confused? So am I. In the minutes of the General Meeting dated 23rd February 1932 Mr G. Walker is named as Bandmaster with Mr Hainsworth as Assistant Bandmaster!

Mr Lambeth was approached in 1930 with a view to him taking the band to contests. This started an association with the band and the Lambeth name that was to span very many decades. Many of the past members whose memories appear at the back of this book have made reference to Mr Les Lambeth, brother of another Lambeth, Mr A. Lambeth. I am unsure as to whether they are connected to this Mr H. Lambeth.

Mr Lambeth lead the band to great success in the Burley in Wharfedale Contest. The band took 1st Place (winning 30 guineas and a cup) and individual players took 4 medals – Mr Hall (Cornet), Mr McEwan (Trombone), Mr Scaife (Euphonium) and Mr Bristow (Horn). Under his direction the band also took 1st Prize in the Bridlington Contest and 3rd Prize at the Crystal Palace Contest in the same year.

Among the many pieces of music purchased during this year was the theme from the new musical film 'Singing in the Rain'.

In 1931 Easingwold Band suffered the loss of their instruments through a fire. Our band committee determined to offer to help raise funds for new instruments. It was put to the Band who agreed unanimously to this but it is not recorded if they actually ended up doing anything to help.

In 1932 the Band had been in existence for 29 years. Curiously, this was the year it was agreed to present Messrs E.E. Sutton and T. Buckle with a *'token of appreciation for their 21 years service with the band'*. Mr Sutton (a founding member of the band) was considered to be *'a loyal and faithful bandsman and a keen worker for the welfare of the band'* – he was presented with a clock. Mr Buckle *'a real artiste on his instrument and a good bandsman and committee man'* who had been solo trombone for 20 years, received an extending dining room table. The following year, 1933, Mr C. Ward received his presentation (a Westminster chime clock) for the completion of 21 years services with the band and was described as *'a most conscientious bandsman'*.

It is obvious in the minutes of February 1934 that the band's fortunes during 1933 were a vast improvement on the previous year's. Singled out for praise was Mr L. Fawcett. His 'Get your Clods ready' fund had raised a fantastic sum of over £6. I am reliably informed by Mr H. Humphrey that a 'clod' in this context refers to an old penny. Bandsmen would pay their clod into a weekly raffle and a prize was given out to the winner. 1932 also saw the band audition at the request of the BBC, but unfortunately their playing was deemed unsuitable for broadcasting purposes.

Whilst the band was on the up financially during 1934, the bandmaster Mr Walker was of the opinion that the playing was going down. To be fair nightshifts and night classes seemed to be the main reason for absences, but, as has been pointed out to bands through the ages - you can't rehearse empty chairs. Mr Walker was in doubt that the band was not in contesting form at this time. They did however play a huge number of concerts, for dancing and for charity. The standard of playing must have improved as they did go along to the Crystal Palace Contest. Sadly they came 17th . There was no record of how many competitors took part. Perhaps Mr Walker had been correct.

I am sure it wasn't a case of 'sour grapes' when the band formally complained to their hotel about the catering (specifically the breakfast they were served on the contest day). There were also unhappy at not receiving any preference for a rehearsal room.

So another New Year 1935 and a new professional conductor is appointed, Mr Noel Thorpe. He had been approached, along with 4 others and was subsequently appointed to give lessons to the band and prepare them for contests. He was to remain the band's professional conductor right through to the start of the Second World War. In the first contest the band entered under his baton, May 1935 – Belle Vue – the band took 1st Place, winning a gold medal for their resident conductor (Mr Walker), the Fifty Guinea Cup and £10. This encouraged the band to enter the July Contest at Belle Vue, in the 2nd Section, when they came 5th out of 16. This was a very good start to this conductors association with the band. Regrettably in the Crystal Palace Contest later in the year the band were 13th out of 26 and out of the prizes.

The sense of a banding community comes out time and again through the minutes. Remember the fire in which Easingwold Band had lost their instruments and our band had been happy to help to raise funds for them. In 1935 the Union of Post Office Workers Band was formed and they wrote to Rowntree's Cocoa Works Band enquiring if we had any music which we did not require. Our band agreed to supply them with some old pieces. Considering the cost of music even then this was an extremely generous response.

When the Joseph Rowntree Theatre opened in 1935, the band was one of the various social sections invited to perform on 4th and 5th November as part of the celebrations.

1936 was a year of very mixed fortunes for the band. There was obvious celebration of contest success – Belle Vue, July – 3rd Place for both the test piece (Ernani) and the March (Elephant).

There was great sadness at the death of Mr A. Lickley, founder of the Cocoa Works band back in 1903. He conducted the band until 1911, when his son G. Lickley took over the baton. His son had been secretary and sometimes treasurer also since the band was formed. Mr A. Lickley (Snr) built up a fine band which was reasonably successful in the world of contesting, entertaining and raising funds for charity. He was a keen and enthusiastic bandsman and was held in the highest esteem by all the bandsmen through his long association. Right up to his death on June 26th 1936, he took a keen interest in the goings on and the welfare of the band. At his very impressive funeral service which was held at Clifton Chapel, the band played his favourite hymns and afterwards the band marched at the head of the Cortege to York Cemetery. *'He loved his band and his band loved him.'*

A second death during this year, Mr Jake Webster, further saddened the band. Mr Webster had been an enthusiastic member of the committee who was always interested in the fortunes of the men. Mr Webster was considered to be a true friend of the band.

Presentations were made to L. Fawcett and H. Wreghitt for their long service to the band. Mr Fawcett received a Westminster chimes clock and was hailed for his loyalty and ingenuity as well as his exceptional abilities as a player (both on cornet and BBb bass). He was for a short while assistant conductor of the band and was equally capable in that role. The presentation which Mr Wreghitt received is not minuted, but it is known that he was also a highly talented musician and very active and vocal member of the band committee.

Later on in the year Mr A. Lickley (Jnr) was presented with a wristlet watch in recognition of his long service having been the band secretary from its inception.

This year saw the attendance at rehearsals slump dramatically due the economic climate of the time. Many of the men were on night shifts or doing overtime. The positive side of this was the state of trade within the works and the security this gave to the men and their families.

However this did not stop the band from gaining 5th Place at the Crystal Palace Contest. The result was all the more remarkable as it was in a higher section than they normally competed in. They were all very proud of this achievement and saw it as a tribute, not only to Mr Walker, the Bandmaster and Mr Thorpe, the Conductor, but also to absent friends.

Out of this success came another chance to audition for the BBC in Leeds during November. Sadly whilst the band was considered good, they were once again considered unsuitable for broadcasting!! They were invited to try again sometime in the future.

Through the minutes of the band committee it is repeatedly noted that within the band there exists good comradeship, teamwork and a very real sense of friendship and loyalty. That holds as true today as it did at any point in the band's history.

CHAPTER 6

Ladies in the bandroom!

Up until now you may have noticed a lack of bandswomen. It is not clear how the subject arose and there is nothing to prepare for it in the minutes prior to the announcement, but… at the General Meeting on 9th November 1936 Mr L. Fawcett proposed and Mr G. Walker seconded that the band should have a LADIES SECTION! There had to be some background to this because the following names were put forward as nominees: Miss Baines, Miss Pickup, Miss Fletcher, Miss Taylor, Miss Weatherill and Miss Crisp. This resolution was agreed and the meeting moved on.

By November 1937 the number of ladies in the Ladies Section had grown to 9, with the addition of Miss Sollitt, Miss Ferguson and Miss Coning. The December 1938 General Meeting details eleven members of the Ladies Section. During the Second World War (1942) the number of ladies went down to 7 and does not seem to have recovered.

In fact after 1942 the Ladies Section is not mentioned again at all in the minutes. What happened? Having discussed the Ladies Section with some past members who were around at the time they have no recollection of there ever having been one. Perhaps it was an experiment that was dropped. Without being able to ask the late Mr G. Lickley, conductor, it seems we will never know. As a bandswoman I am intrigued by this enigma. So if you know any details please let me know.

Having made the momentous step forward of training women to be brass players, it would be a further 18 years before one was enrolled as a member and contested with the band. That lady was Mrs Grace Pratt (nee Dinsdale) who played with the band for a short while following her marriage to Ted Pratt, one of the Solo Cornetists. Grace is mentioned in more detail in the Past Members Section but I couldn't resist a little mention here.

The photograph on the opposite page shows Grace with the band in 1958, following their contest success and also celebrating the band having existed for 55 years:

Back now to the band's story – Coronation Year – 1937.

The band was greatly sought after naturally during this year of celebration.

This was also the year when the Crystal Palace Contest moved out of necessity to the Alexandra Palace. Following the devastating fire that

had caused the closure of the Crystal Palace. Below the photograph which was taken in 1936, showing the band with Mr Walker, conductor, outside the Crystal Palace:

CRYSTAL PALACE 1936 SECTION 3 5ᵗʰPRIZE "PRIDE OF RACE."

It's a little sad to think that this was the last time they would play at the Crystal Palace, having played there year upon year for more than 30 years. Still banding goes on and whilst they didn't win any prizes in the 1937 Alexandra Palace Contest, they did play one of my personal favourites 'Kenilworth' as a test piece.

During 1937, as well as events connected with the Coronation celebrations, the band fulfilled a number of engagements and contests which had become a tradition for them e.g. Whit Monday (Otley). This was the 11th year that they had contested here. It was also their 8th appearance at the York Cattle Show, a prestigious venue (despite the country smells). They continued with their charity concerts for local causes such as Selby Hospital and fulfilled engagements for York Corporation to boot. They even managed a concert at Alton Towers. Below are photographs of some of the bandsmen relaxing between performances and the band preparing to play at this delightful venue.

The band also held another dance, something which had become a tradition, along with the whist drives and the now infamous Clod Fund. Another coup was playing at the International Aviation Meeting at York Aerodrome. Also the band held a celebration concert in the Joseph Rowntree Theatre.

All in all this was a very pleasant year in the band's history, making music and money.

The following year 1938 passed just as pleasantly, perhaps with less money being made and a few less concerts, but even so no hint of what was just around the corner, the Second World War. They were planning the purchase of some new instruments which were badly needed – a euphonium, Eb Bass and Flugel Horn. The firm was to be approached to see what financial help could be given. The band played at Otley again (12th time) and held 2 Variety Shows in Joseph Rowntree Theatre.

The preparation for the Variety Shows indicates the content planned for each performance. The following were agreed (provisionally) at the meeting on 3rd March 1938: The Rowntree Band would play, N. Holmes and his band would also play and there would be an accordion solo. There would also be a Comic Band (doing sketches), someone playing the Ukulele, our own Mr Medley (comedian) and all these would be interspersed with instrumental solos, duets and quartets. It really sounds very entertaining, and was such a success that a second concert was organised.

I have neglected to mention before now that the band held frequent solo and quartet competitions amongst themselves. These were annual occasions and were handled very sensibly. All members were required to play a solo. The quartet groups had to play a standard piece and they were handicapped, thus preventing all the best players grouping together and having an advantage. In 1938 the adjudicator was Mr A. Lickley (Jnr), the band secretary who had never been a playing member but whose opinion was obviously highly regarded. The handicapper for the quartet competition was the bandmaster Mr Walker. This seems an extremely fair way to encourage bandsmen to improve their playing and give entertainment at the same time.

The band was placed 3rd at the Belle Vue Contest and additionally received the deportment prize, which was considered by the secretary to be of equal importance (but then he wasn't a player, was he). He felt it was a great credit to the band and only unfortunate that we were unplaced in the Selection Contest!

Alexandra Palace was left off the list of contests the band competed in during 1938 at the request of the members but the secretary had it in mind for the following year along with Leeds, Manchester, and the purchase of those much-needed instruments.

So finally in November 1938, it was agreed to purchase 2 cornets, 1 tenor horn, 1 baritone, 1 euphonium, 2 Eb basses and 2 BBb Basses. The difference between what the band could pay and the cost would be met by a 10-year loan from the firm. However, it was minuted that the band should pay as much as possible in the first instance in order to reduce the level of the loan. It was agreed to have a representative from the instrument manufacturers to come down with a view to purchasing the old instruments.

During February 1939 the band committee were busy discussing the usual issues, new overcoats, changes of instruments for players desiring so to do, contest and concerts.

From this point we have no record of any minutes of meetings until February 1942. Still there was banding being done during part of 1939 (war wasn't declared until September). The band carried out a full list of engagements, as various as in previous years. They included their 13th visit to Otley (Whit Monday), St Peters' School Engine Ceremony in York Station, Alton Towers, a fantastically profitable Variety Show in Joseph Rowntree Theatre, the York Cattle Show (Fat Stock Show) and the Belle Vue Contest. At the Belle Vue Contest they won no prize for music, but won the deportment prize. The Alexandra Palace Contest was postponed due to the declaration of war.

CHAPTER

7

During the war years the band did all they could to keep going. It was difficult but many members made enormous efforts to ensure that the band continued, after a fashion, as follows:

The first concert given, after the declaration of war was in the Centenary Canteen and Club – for Soldiers.

During 1940 the band performed for the Cocoa Works Sports and did a Sunday Evening Concert in Joseph Rowntree Theatre. They played twice for the Centenary Soldiers Club and also played twice at the YMCA Hut on St George's Field. September and December saw them take part in the Home Guard church parade to New Earswick and December also saw 4 Trumpeters (from the band members) play Tertius Noble's 'York Pageant Fanfare' at the opening of the Red Cross Bazaar (on the Friday and Saturday). There were two Variety Concerts given in Joseph Rowntree Theatre in aid of our Gallant Seaman. The proceeds were divided between 'Minesweepers' (£18:18:0), HMS York (£2) and the Royal Life Boat Institution (£2:2:0). They also contributed £2:2:0 to York's 'Spitfire' Fund. This would be considered an amazing number of engagements at any time how much more commendable during a war.

The band was always full of ingenious and inventive ways of raising funds and two that I particularly like the sound of happened during March 1941. In the Centenary Club and Canteen the band organised 'Name the Tunes (& count the number of them) in a musical medley. They also held a 'Conduct the Band' which proved a huge success and four soldiers and a lady ATS wielded the baton. The following month they visited Blackburn Aircraft Factory (Sherburn-in-Elmet). The factory paid for the bus to transport the band to this venue.

During May 1941 was a designated 'War Weapons Week'. The band played on the Sunday in Rowntree Park, and on the Wednesday and Saturday they played in the Museum Gardens. The Lord Mayor announced the results of the week at the Mansion House. The band had marched there on the Saturday after their performance in the Gardens in time for the announcement. Later that month another concert was given in the Centenary Canteen for Soldiers.

July saw the band play (their instruments) at York City Football Ground for a physical training display. Do you remember how long they tried to get the park for a concert?

A diversion from the brass band scene was made to aid the war effort by 5 of the members. They formed a highly successful quintet and played dance music to lift the spirits of the community.

The picture below was taken in the large hall in the dining block of Rowntree's Factory. It shows a merry bunch of musicians who entertained at dances and fundraising events throughout the war. Johnny went on to form his own dance band and continued with it for years whilst continuing to play with the brass band.

Left to right:Les Lambeth / Ted Sutton / unknown / Johnny Sutton / Bill Humphrey

In 1942, the band got off to a great start. The minutes of the General Meeting (23.2.42) record that they have made enough money to pay off the loan for new instruments in less than three years instead of the expected ten.

This year several of the band members were presented with gifts on completion of over 21 years service. They were described collectively as *'good bandsmen who have been faithful to the band through its trials and successes. All were looking forward to the time when the band will once again be active in the contest field and resume our pleasant relationship with our friends, connected with the many engagements attended by the band'.* Those members were:

Arthur Bristow, Arthur and Ernest Dobson, Edward Fawcett, Albert Slater, Edward A. Sutton, Charles Winter and William Woodcock. As a wartime measure only each of the above was allocated £5 in lieu of a gift.

Gifts of cash were also sent to each of the bandsmen who were currently serving in the armed forces. Members subscribed 3d (about 1p these days) each week. Mr Humphrey was charged with stewarding this gift and canvassing members.

Throughout this war, as in the Great War the bandroom was routinely opened every Monday and Thursday to *enable any members who could to come along to a rehearsal at least once per week on average.* There were members of the band on active duty, they aren't named in the minutes, naturally they were in the thoughts of those left behind who all wished them a speedy and safe return.

The secretary praised the musical and social value of the band and emphasised that its very existence depended upon the interest displayed by each member without whose co-operation the band would wither and die. Despite the low attendances during this period all were optimistic enough to believe that they were keeping the band together for better times – how right they were. It's impossible to overestimate the contribution made by these men and so many others to the life of this band. They are our past and without them the band would not have had a future.

There was an average of only 6 or 7 men attending rehearsals even though the available membership was 18 playing members. It has to be said that the war effort was the single reason for the majority of the member's irregular attendance and it is difficult, if not impossible, to be critical of that.

In July 1945 the persistent absenteeism of a certain few members was giving cause for concern (understandable really as one of them was a member of the previously mentioned dance band!). The secretary was instructed to write to each of them (Messrs Bruce, Turner, J. Sutton and A. Lambeth) in order to establish their position regarding attendance at band rehearsals. In the end Mr Bruce resigned, owing to the nature of his work he found it impracticable to attend rehearsals regularly. Mr A.

Lambeth explained that the war work that he was performing together with travelling had prevented him from attending practises but that he would make every effort to attend as often as possible. Mr J. Sutton replied that he had interested himself in another form of band and tendered his resignation. This was eventually accepted.

There is no record of a reply being received from Mr Turner, however Mr Gibson also tendered his resignation at this time. Mr E. Fawcett explained that he was having some trouble with his teeth and it was agreed that he should return as soon as his teeth would permit him to play.

It was not all doom and gloom though, new members were applying to join and members of the juniors were being invited to join the Senior band to make up numbers. By October 1945 the band consisted of 17 playing members which included learners. Considering the times it was generally accepted that attendances and membership were as good as they could be. Low numbers did cause the band to turn down several of the engagements that had become part of the band's regular work. This was deeply regretted but unavoidable. One such engagement was the Remembrance Day in Selby. It was hoped that a deal of understanding would be used and that these engagements would not be lost forever.

There were two more resignations during the October 1945 meeting, Mr G. Walker (bandmaster) and Mr A. Lickley (Jnr). Mr Walker had written to the committee tendering his resignation. He had given very careful consideration to his decision but owing to extra duties that had been placed upon him, he felt he had no other alternative. In paying tribute to Mr Walker, Mr Lickley referred to the hard work that Mr Walker had performed for the band. Many members of the band agreed with these kind words and it was agreed that some form of present should be given as a token of the band's appreciation for all that Mr Walker had done.

Another blow to the band committee came with the resignation of the band's secretary, Mr A. Lickley (Jnr). Mr Lickley was retiring from business and would eventually be moving away from York. He did agree however to carry on until his retirement came into operation. Mr Lickley had been Secretary of Rowntree Band since its inception and had carried out those demanding duties ungrudgingly. All that he did was always done for the betterment of the band. Those members at the meeting agreed that this decision was deeply regretted by all present and as before it was agreed that a suitable retirement gift should be sought. It was also agreed that a public acknowledgement of Mr Lickley's record whilst associated with Rowntree's Band should be made.

At the same meeting 5 new members were proposed, seconded and instated as new players, 2 others were left over. This had been a really long meeting and at this point a break was called and the meeting was set to reconvene the following week to continue discussing the business of the band.

So here we are one week on and another resignation is tendered. This time it is the band Chairman, Mr Rayson. Due to his nearing retirement he had tendered his resignation and it was agreed that a letter of appreciation be sent to him, thanking him for the work he had done for the band and the interest he had taken in it.

Mr Lickley reported to this meeting that, as yet, he had no success in his endeavours to find his own replacement. He felt that there was no need to hurry, at least for the time being. He was sure the post would be satisfactorily filled.

Filling the bandmaster's post was a more pressing issue. It was suggested by Dr Northcote that Mr L. Lambeth be given a 6 months trial to see if he liked the post and for the members to judge if they liked him as a Bandmaster. Mr Lambeth had been Assistant Bandmaster since 1937 and he had been a playing member long before this time so he was well known to the bandsmen. However it was felt that it would be more correct for Mr Lambeth to remain as Assistant Bandmaster and take rehearsals until the next General Meeting. This action was in accordance with the rules of the band.

The Treasurer's post would be treated similarly with the agreement that Mr Walker's name should be put forward at the General Meeting.

At least the Learners were being looked after seamlessly. Mr L. Lambeth had undertaken to take them following Mr Walker's retirement.

CHAPTER 8

So, the Second World War had finally ended and the band held the first post war General Meeting on 17th January 1946.

There were 15 playing members in attendance and Mr E. Dobson had the chair. They spent a deal of time recapping on the band's activities during the early part of the war and regretting that the numbers had been so affected by members serving both at home and abroad. The savings scheme to send money to those serving in the forces had also dwindled to a negligible amount and it was hoped that those members would understand the difficulties being faced at home.

The band was delighted to welcome back those who had recently returned from the War: Teddy Sutton and Harry Pawson. The band was thankful that they had come through their trying experiences and were once more able to enjoy the musical recreation and companionship of the band. Charlie Winter was still on active service and Norman Kilvington was at Morpeth, pending his imminent discharge.

W. Stephenson had not been heard from since the previous August but Leon Walker was at Bulford and hoped to return to the works on his release from the Forces.

During 1944 the band had received many applications from apprentices to join the band and our stalwart, Mr Walker, had taken them in hand. In the midst of the darkest days these young enthusiasts were very helpful in keeping the music going along with the assistance of others. The band had been hopeful that these young men would prove to be a great asset and fill the gaps that were too evident within the band. Unfortunately, several of them had also been called up. It was hoped that their short stay would be sufficient to foster a love of good music and that, on their return, they would still be interested in the band.

Best wishes were sent to all those absent members, wherever they might be.

In summarising the inter war years, mention was made of the quantity of music which was purchased. It was hoped that this would create additional interest in the band and that the band would be ready with something interesting to perform to the 'boys' on their return to civilian life.

Mr Walker's resignation as bandmaster was mentioned and it was noted that he had expressed interest in being the band treasurer. Mr L. Lambeth had been responsible for the band, in his capacity as Deputy Bandmaster and thanks were given to him for filling the breach so well.

The band ended the war in a very healthy financial position – having amassed £77:17:3 in the bank and a further £77:1:3 in the Rowntree & Co. account – giving an impressive total of £154:18:6.

Having firmly disposed of the business carried out through the war years the band meeting settled down to discuss and prepare for the future.

Subscriptions, band rules, music and contests were all discussed as were 2 further applications for 21 years Long Service – by J. Sutton and Mr Gibson. It was agreed to gift £5 to Mr J. Sutton, and also to approach him with a view to continuing as a member. Mr Gibson was a slightly different case, there was some doubt that he had, at this point, completed his 21 years and so his situation was left over to allow for the facts to be established.

Finally this first meeting ended perhaps with a whist drive although that's not actually mentioned.

The first available contest was the Daily Herald Contest. It was thought that the band was not yet in a position to enter the contesting arena and so the secretary (now Mr Humphrey) was asked to write and inform the contest committee of this. The same course was chosen regarding the Ossett Contest, but the hope of contesting again in the future was there as the band agreed to join the West Riding Band Association.

What was important to the band now that the war had ended was to hold a Reunion Dinner. Members' wives were to be invited and members were to pay for themselves, however, the band would pay for those who had returned from the Forces. The venue selected was the Granby Lodge Hotel and the cost would be 6/6 (32.5p) per head. The date was fixed for 9th November 1946.

The Reunion Dinner was chosen as the appropriate time to make presentations to the retiring bandmaster, Mr G. Lickley and also the retiring secretary, Mr A. Lickley (Jnr). Both these gentlemen can be seen at the top table at this gathering. The fashion worn by the ladies

The photograph above is of a band dinner, I have not been able to establish if it is the actual reunion dinner or not.

also leans towards the post war era. Two good reasons for assuming this maybe the Reunion Dinner photograph.

The band settled down to giving concerts – to the Youth Club, at the Pocklington Show and also one for the Magic Circle.

There was concern that two members, Mr A. Lambeth and Mr Walker (not ex-bandmaster) had not been attending rehearsals. It was proposed that the secretary write to them and ask them to confirm that they were still members of the band. As a result Mr A. Lambeth had replied and placed his resignation in the hands of the committee. Mr Walker wished to remain a member and in the near future he was certain he would be able to devote much more of his time to the band. The committee accepted both these replies.

A Mr Fairclough (BBb Bass) wanted to join the band at the end of 1946 provided a situation with the firm as a fitter could be obtained. The Secretary was instructed to do all he could in this direction. Once again the ability to play an instrument could help a man get employment in those days.

The following year (1947) saw the band once again lead the parade at the New Earswick Carnival for the first time since the war and then provide music on the sports field. The band became members of the West Riding Brass Band Society (WRBBS) and took part in the WRBBS contest, held at Rowntrees on 1st February. The band took 4th Prize. This was considered a fantastic result and had been achieved without the use of borrowed players to improve the numbers. This was a hugely successful contest, accommodated in the Rowntree Hall and was supported by record attendances. The Lord Mayor attended the concert the band gave later in the week in cooperation with the Magic Circle on February 5th.

The Daily Herald Contest took place on 15th March and once again the band battled against numerical odds but retained prestige by gaining 5th place in the awards.

The band took part in a service in the Minster on 4th May, along with the other York bands and Mr Francis Jackson conducted them and the choir for this grand occasion.

A succession of concerts punctuated the bands calendar including one for the Youth Club, another for an unnamed girls school and its teachers, a concert on Rowntrees Sports Field and the York Agricultural Show. During August and September the band gave seven lunch hour concerts on the Time Office Rose Lawn and was appreciated by a large number of employees, some of them had not realised the band existed.

The year was concluded by attendance at the WRBBS in Cleakheaton, on 22nd November in which the band was disappointingly awarded 4th Prize. It was decided to attend this contest supplementing the reduced ranks of the band with two borrowed players from Bradford Victoria Band (a euphonium and a BBb Bass) and also to go with Mr L. Lambeth as the bandmaster and not engage a professional conductor.

During this year the band bought new 'Kosicup' mouthpieces for the cornets and purchased several new pieces of music. They tendered for work at the Bishopthorpe Garden Fete, the Brough Show and offered a reduced price to the Agricultural Show as the proceeds were for the Flood Relief Fund. They also quoted for an engagement at the Masham Agricultural Show which they attended and had a thoroughly pleasant day out, re-igniting the previous travelling spirit which had existed prior to the war.

A new drum was needed (preferably one with rod-tension) and some overcoats had been spotted at £3:1:9:6 each. To get enough for the entire band was to be expensive and so the secretary was asked to see if some financial assistance could be obtained from the firm in this matter. A new soprano cornet was also wanted and 3 were requested from Kitchens of Leeds, for trial. In the end a Besson & Co. Soprano and case were selected at a cost of £44:8:3. For the first time, cornet mutes were bought for the cornet section, they cost 11/6 each and were supplied by Besson & Co.

The Bandmaster was especially proud of the achievements of our youngest member – Peter Mortimer. Peter had won the Juniors Senior section and a medal at the British Legion Slow Melody Contest.

There had been a suggestion that the band might make a recording. However the price quoted to them seemed to be too expensive. The subject was broached again and this time less opposition was met and so the secretary and bandmaster were asked to pursue it. It was felt necessary by the Post Office band to call a meeting of the York bands in order to agree a minimum rate for York Corporation engagements. Our band suggested a minimum fee of £20 for a single performance and £25 for a double one.

The band was looking ahead and upwards by ordering both the 1st and 2nd Section Test Pieces for the following year's Daily Herald Contest although they planned to enter the 2nd Section contest (and came 5th).

The plans to record the band were moving along and the committee agreed to supply an augmented band and bear the cost of the extra players if the firm would finance the recording. It doesn't seem to have come to anything though, as there is no further mention within the minutes.

In the meantime there was the 1948 Bishop Wilton Show to quote for and also a performance in Halifax Park. Another York Agricultural show was on the cards and a new venture to Whitby Flower Show was being tendered for, at the Show organisers' behest. The band also took part in the Manchester Belle Vue Contests.

In fact 1948 was reported as one of the busiest and most successful years in the history of the Cocoa Works Band. Special reference was made in the February 1949 General Meeting to the two concerts given in the Joseph Rowntree Theatre at which the St Lawrence Male Voice Choir took part. This combination of band and voice proved to be successful and appealed to the public. The May Belle Vue contest saw the band gaining 2nd Prize (out of 22 competitors). In the June Belle Vue Contest the band got another 2nd Prize (but this time it was for deportment) and they got 4th Prize in the March. It is reported that this kept up our record of having secured a prize on every occasion that the band had competed at Belle Vue.

The lunchtime concerts on the Rose Lawn numbered thirteen during 1948 compared with six the previous year, leaving no doubt as to the popularity of these concerts. Many engagements had been fulfilled and the band had enhanced its reputation whilst doing them from both a musical point of view and also in deportment. The bandmaster wondered if fewer contests should be participated in so that the music at rehearsals could be more varied and interesting and would then perhaps encourage better attendances throughout the year. It was discouraging to the regular attendees when other players were seen less often at rehearsals.

One Long Service presentation was made during 1949 and that was to Mr H. Humphrey for 21 years service to the band. It was agreed that he should receive *'the usual present'*.

Interestingly, at the General Meeting on 10th February 1949 gambling was one of the subjects. There was a proposal that gambling should be permitted when travelling in a bus. After a lengthy discussion it was agreed that this subject was closed!

Good sense was starting to prevail regarding members helping out other groups of musicians. After all since the war it had been necessary on several occasions to 'borrow' players from willing bands. So when Mr E. Fawcett asked for permission to 'play out' it was agreed that he could attend, with the band's G Trombone, three performances with the York Symphony Orchestra. This was no longer an issue provided it did not interfere with the plans of the Rowntree band.

What was the band planning when it quoted £20 for two performances or £15 for a single one to York Corporation, for playing in the Corporation Parks? Hadn't there been an agreement with the York bands (see previous page) that they would all charge the same? A curious point that appears in the minutes in March 1949 but remains unexplained. The quote was accepted incidentally!

At the same meeting Masters P. Pawson and F. Dawson were made members, *'without the need for the usual application'*. I assume they had been learners previously and therefore were well known to the band. F. Dawson appears towards the end of the book in the Past Members Section as he was to be a member on and off over a period of 51 years.

Sadly the band lost another of its friends this year – Mr W.C. Woodcock – a hard working member of the band and loyal committee man for many years. A wreath was sent to his funeral on behalf of the band.

Uniforms for the Juniors was discussed during March 1949 so they must have either been accompanying the Band on outings or were performing in their own right at some point. There is little elaboration within the archives to explain why else they might require a uniform. The first firm to be contacted, Beevers, was not able to match the same coloured cloth as the Senior Band uniform and so the Secretary (Mr L. Lambeth) was asked to approach Evans.

The Wednesday Lunchtime Lawn Concerts were reviewed by Dr Macdonald, one of the band Presidents. In his opinion they had been much appreciated and should continue in the months between June and September. The main objection which band members had to these concerts was obvious. It was difficult to get a good representative band and there was also the question of time off. So, rather than do one every fortnight it was proposed to carry out three over the summer period and that the band should wear uniform and each member be recommended for time-off with respect to the distance the Rose Lawn was from the Works. Dr Macdonald also agreed to look into the question of supplying waste sweets to non-Rowntrees & Co members of the band!

Prior to the Filey Contest of 1949, a practice room had been offered in Humanby and if the bus were to leave York at 8 am then the rehearsal could begin at 10 am. We have a similar habit these days of getting a hall, either in a school or somewhere nearby our contest, and holding a short rehearsal, just to steady the nerves.

Mr Drabwell resigned in May 1949 and it was felt that the secretary should approach him to ascertain his motive for resigning as that hadn't been made clear to the committee. At the same time the band needed a cornet for Mr Plows and it was hoped that one might be purchased from the Besson stand (if they had one) whilst at the Filey Contest. The said cornet was not purchased at Filey, as it was thought that an agent in Newcastle would be able to get hold of one and it was left with the bandmaster to liaise with him as they were acquainted.

This contest in Filey was notable in that the set test piece that the band played was performed extremely well, according to the adjudicator on the day, however, it was the wrong arrangement and therefore the band could not be included in the prizes. I would not like to have been on the bus back from that contest. At the next General Meeting in February 1950 it was noted that *'our only appearance at a contest in 1949 was marred by a very unfortunate experience which, the secretary had no doubt, had taught a few of our officials to be extremely wary in the future'*. I would consider that comment a mild understatement – wouldn't you?

June 1949 saw the band in communication with Mr H. Mortimer (a world famous musician and teacher). The band wished to engage him for two lessons and a dinnertime concert on 19th, 20th and 21st July. Further communication saw Mr Mortimer arrange for the band to have a BBC audition at the works, with Mr Mortimer and Mr Johnstone. These arrangements, as with most things, were left in the hands of Mr Lambeth, the bandmaster.

The committee came under intense criticism for the first time during the General Meeting at the start of 1950. The Chairman said, in his report to the band *'the past year has been a year which I regret has been full of mixed happenings and I feel that from an administrative angle we have not got the best out of the material we have as members of the band and certainly we have not maintained the high standards in executive positions which have been peculiar to R & C Band. I speak with much feeling when I say that the Secretary, as much as I admire him for his enthusiasm in taking on the job, has allowed it to drift into a state which has been the cause of many complaints and has caused other members to commit themselves and assume beliefs that are not consistent with the high standard of efficiency. At all times I have advocated democracy, a term which I construe to mean that my duty is to represent the majority of the members. Whether their views are my views or not, I must stand for common democracy'*. It wasn't all bad news, honestly, the Chairman had kind words and encouraging remarks for individuals and the band in general, but it was obvious that the year had been very frustrating for him.

Mr Dobson continued *'At this moment, all last years officers are without office, all positions are subject to this meeting and I hope your wisdom will bear fruit and let the past year be gone and tomorrow start anew'*. Mr Dobson went on to pay tribute to Peter Mortimer, an excellent cornetist who was to hold the position of principal cornet for over 30 years. No other principal has even come close to that record before or since Mr Mortimer's time. Mr Dobson was glad to have seen so much of Mr A. Lickley (Jnr) over the past year and was ever pleased to have the benefit of his wise counsel.

The oldest member, Mr E.E. Sutton who was still on the 'Active List' came in for special praise.

In 1950 the still weakened band managed a 5th Prize at the new Yorkshire Areas Contest and won £2 at the Belle Vue Contest. Given that membership was low it was noted that some instruments were being recovered from members who attended insufficient rehearsals.

Replacement uniforms were back on the agenda and Mr Humphrey (Assistant Secretary, with special responsibility for liasing with the company) was asked to discuss this matter with Dr Macdonald. It was estimated that the necessary uniforms would total around £450. A bit of a hike from the first set, which, if you remember came to £48.20 (including caps!). Dr Macdonald's response was that the matter should be brought up at a more opportune time. In the meantime he intimated that he would like to inspect the uniforms perhaps at the Sports engagement. As a result of this decision the secretary was asked to inform the Army & Navy Stores & Beevers that this question would not be dealt with for some months.

Six months later Dr Macdonald wrote to the band asking if they would be prepared to put up £100 towards to cost of the new uniforms and for the money to be paid up over 5 years. The secretary was instructed to write to Dr Macdonald and accept his proposal.

The colour of uniforms was mentioned for the first time – the original colour had been maroon and it was thought that it might be nice to have a change. So Beevers were asked to make up two uniforms – one in blue and one in maroon. These were ready during September, 1950 and after considerable debate the band committee chose the maroon uniform. The following year the old uniforms were sold to the Ebenezer Baptist Church Band for the princely sum of £150.

A xylophone was purchased late in 1950. Besson and Co had contacted the band earlier in the year as they had a second hand xylophone for sale at £35. After having it for a trial period the band agreed to buy it.

The band said goodbye to the Pawson family at the end of 1950. Mr Pawson had been a member of the band for a long time and his sons had only recently progressed from the Learners Band. The family were emigrating to Australia and the band decided to purchase three Fountain Pens, one costing £4:6:2 and two others costing £1:10:7 each. They were engraved and presented at the annual band dinner. A Testimonial was also given to each of them. This was, in effect, a bandsman's reference – a nice idea and it would be useful to have this sometimes, nowadays.

Once again, in preparation for the March Area Contest, the committee decided to purchase both the 1st and 2nd Section Test Pieces. The 1st Section piece was 'Atlantic' and it was bought without the score. 'English Maiden' was the 2nd Section test piece and the score was bought for this one.

Having made such a successful deal with the sale of the old uniforms, it was proposed in 1951 to sell off some of the older instruments as well. The band needed a new euphonium and they were too expensive, so Besson & Co offered to trade the old instruments in for a second hand euphonium. They valued the old instruments at £67 but would give £75 for them provided a new case was bought for the euphonium. Whilst waiting for written confirmation of this deal the committee decided to ask a representative from Kitchens to come along and look at the old instruments. This rep. offered to buy all nine of the old instruments for £100. The band accepted this offer and paid Besson & Co £144:19:6 for the euphonium.

In view of the unsatisfactory fit of the new uniforms, the secretary wrote to Beevers asking for the representative to come along to the band room with a view to effecting the necessary alterations. Given the trouble the band had been to it must have been disappointing for the uniforms to fit badly. They had, as previously mentioned, already sold the old uniforms and they prided themselves on their deportment (they had won deportment prizes at many contests). Still once the alterations were completed these jackets were used for around 12 years.

In 1951 the band carried out a fewer number of engagements and had success at the Yorkshire Area Contest - 5th Prize. Otherwise it was a relatively uneventful year with 4 lunchtime concerts being given on the Rose Lawn, an engagement (for the first time) at the June Caravan Rally. The Remembrance Day Service at Selby was again a regular engagement for the band as was the fundraiser in Homestead Park. Homestead Park was a financial let down on this occasion and it was felt that the amount being raised here no longer merited the band playing (only £4 was collected and then expenses had to be deducted). The Annual Dinner in the City Arms Hotel was a great success as was the Annual Outing from York to Scarborough via Whitby.

It was suggested that help should be given to our 'boy' members with a view to obtaining work with the firm and Mr Humphrey offered to discuss this issue with Dr Macdonald.

The bandmaster, Mr L. Lambeth, was not satisfied with the attendances at practices and emphasised the need for a marked improvement in this direction. If this was not carried out he indicated that he would have to reconsider his position as bandmaster.

As the General Meeting of February 1952 got underway, the main item on the agenda was how to celebrate the band's Golden Jubilee. There was no doubt surrounding the fact that the band will have been in existence for 50 years during 1953 and in the view of the band members, something should be done to celebrate the occasion.

Several suggestions were made and it was agreed that a special meeting should be held in July to consider the celebration plans. In the meantime it was agreed that November 1953 would be a suitable month for the celebrations and members were asked to put forward suggestions which would contribute to making it a great success.

CHAPTER 9

1952 saw the band come 5th again at the Yorkshire Area (Daily Herald) Contest. The preparations for the band's Golden Jubilee were augmented by another celebration – the Coronation of Queen Elizabeth II. It must have been a trying year, attempting to focus on two huge events for the band. However with their usual enthusiasm and the opportunity to boost band funds, the band accepted as many requests for engagements as they could manage.

The Golden Jubilee Celebrations:

Well unbelievably there were still three members of the original 1903 band associated with this 1953 band. They were Mr A. Lickley (Jnr), Mr G. Walker and finally Mr E.E. Sutton (who was still an active playing member). All of these men were awarded 50 Years Certificates for their Service with Brass Bands by the Brass Band Association. This was a truly remarkable achievement. For any band of this era to have one man who served for 50 years was amazing, but here we were with three of them, and all founder members of the band, just wonderful. Below is a newspaper clipping of the time, showing a similar presentation that was made a few years later to celebrate another triple 50 year celebration with Mr E.A Sutton (E.E. Sutton's son), Mr E. Dobson and Mr L. Bilham.

A century and a half of umpa-pah were celebrated at the Punch Bowl Hotel, Lowther Street, York, last night, when three members of 50 years' standing in the Rowntree Mackintosh works band received presentations.

The oldest member was Mr. Ernest Dobson, aged 70, of 29 Hobgate, York, who plays the double bass and received a watch. Mrs. Edward Sutton, aged 63, of 42 Usher Lane, Haxby, plays the euphonium and received a pair of binoculars. Mr. Leonard Billham, aged 62, of 22 Edgware Road, York, played the horn for many years but recently graduated to the baritone. He received a silver tea service.

Making the presentations were Mr. R. W. Whitelock and Mr. A. D. S. Robertson, of Rowntree Mackintosh, who were among 60 people at the social evening.

Our picture shows Mr. Peter Mortimer, chairman of the band, with (from the left): Mr. Dobson, Mr. Sutton, and Mr. Bilham.

Oh yes there was a Coronation happening as well wasn't there. The band was engaged to play at Muncaster's Coronation Celebrations and at an event for Wakefield Council. At an average charge of £40 per performance, the band was doing just fine thank you. Just as well really because there was no reduction in the number of concerts the band did to raise funds for local charities. The Lord Mayor's Fund was a favourite of the band, this year the money was to aid the Flood Disaster Fund. The Lord Mayor was invited to attend.

There were plenty of contests around as well in 1953, although I can't tell if they just attended or actually competed in the following, The Daily Herald Contest in Selby; The Huddersfield Contest and a contest in Leicester. Various remarks in the minutes lead me to believe that the band may well have competed but I haven't been able to find any results for these contests, sorry, if you know what went on, please let me know.

The General Meeting of the band during February 1953 highlighted the advantages of doing well at contests and the publicity that it gave the band, in this year of celebration. The death of two of the players was reported at this meeting – Mr L. Fawcett and Mr H. Lambeth (who did so much for the band). Mr Fawcett was a great loss to the band as he had always been a willing player and active committeeman. The members stood in silence as a mark of appreciation and sympathy. The secretary wished to expand further and said *'It was with regret to me and all the members of the band to learn of the loss of our old friend L. Fawcett. He was an untiring worker for our band and proved to be one of our outstanding players. With your permission, gentlemen, I would like to place on record our high appreciation for the valuable services he gave to Rowntrees Band'*. As for Mr H. Lambeth, the secretary continued by saying *'of our old friend and late professional Conductor – he lived for brass bands and after becoming inactive as a conductor he still maintained his interests in the brass band movement'*.

The meeting informed the band that Mr L. Lambeth, bandmaster, had had a successful audition for the position of resident bandmaster with Faireys (still a terrific band). Whilst he did not accept the post, it was pleasing to the band to learn this information.

So the band was set for a busy year, lots of Coronation work, the contests and Lunchtime Concerts and charitable concerts such as the annual engagement at Fairfield Sanatorium. The social side of the band was not being neglected either, a band dinner was set for the Saturday following the Jubilee Concert in November. Two photographs of this band dinner were purchased (maybe the Reunion Dinner photograph should actually be the Golden Jubilee Dinner photograph – sadly those that I've asked are unsure which it is so I've left it where it is).

Even with all of these events going on the band had problems turning out a full set of musicians for the many engagements. The works were flourishing and shift work and overtime were eating into the availability of players. All the time though, Mr L. Lambeth was working hard with the Learners Group producing good musicians to join the Senior Band. Frequently men wishing to join approached the band. Sometimes they were eminently suitable, other times they were not. Perhaps two out of every three who applied were of a standard to be offered a seat and even then that would only be offered as a permanent place after one months trial and if a suitable vacancy was available within the band.

The Jubilee Concert was to be in two halves, one hour each in length. The band would play for one hour and the 'Ballet Dancers of "Georgina"' would be allotted one hour also. The cost of tickets was 1/6 or 1/-. It was hoped that the compere would be Mr F. Lawson, but if he was unavailable a Mr Atkinson was to be asked.

The Chairman of the band wanted Dr Macdonald to be able to present the 50 Years Certificates to Messrs Lickley, Walker and Sutton at the Band Dinner in November and asked that he say a few words first. There is a picture of that occasion, below, showing Dr Macdonald making a presentation to Mr G. Walker with Mr Sutton behind and Mr Humphrey and Mr Dobson looking on.

Below is the article that appeared in the Cocoa Works magazine in Summer 1953.

1903

Mr. A. Lickley,
Secretary 1903-1945

Back Row, left to right: Messrs. C. Parsons, G. Walker, G. H. Foote (Asst. Hon. Sec.), F. Jackson, R. H. Anderson, J. Oglesby, W. Kettlewell.

Middle Row, left to right: Messrs. G. F. Lickley (Deputy Bandmaster), F. R. Gofton, A. Lickley, Junr. (Hon. Sec.), R. Pearson, E. V. Hartley, W. Digeles, H. Ford, E. E. Sutton, J. Purdy, H. Wilson.

Front Row, left to right: Messrs. A. Lickley, Snr. (Bandmaster), W. Lowley, W. Barker, — Horseman, — Catlin, F. Lickley, J. Cattley, E. Cundall, J. Gunnell, T. Stainsby.

THE GOLDEN JUBILEE OF OUR BAND

Mr. A. Lickley, 1903-1911   Mr. G. Lickley, 1911-1927   Mr. W. Hainsworth, 1927-1932   Mr. G. Walker, 1932-1945   Mr. L. Lambeth, 1945

Our warmest congratulations to "Our Band" on the occasion of its Golden Jubilee.

We are proud to note the many public functions in which it takes part and are particularly pleased when it achieves success in band competitions. May the Band long continue to provide enjoyable musical recreation not only for its members but also for the many lovers of brass band music at the Works.

Back Row, left to right: Messrs. R. Walker, W. Stamp, T. Clarke, W. Stephenson, D. Plows, P. Mortimer, G. Eastwood.

Second Row, left to right: Messrs. H. Wreghitt, E. Sutton, Snr., A. Sutton, H. Humphrey, W. Medley, F. Dawson, A. Bristow, T. Eastwood.

Front Row, left to right: Messrs. D. B. Ives, A. Slater, E. Sutton, Junr., N. Kilvington, L. Lambeth (Bandmaster), A. Dobson, E. Dobson, A. Jowrey, E. Jarman.

Mr. H. Humphrey, present Assistant Secretary

1953

Below is the 1953 Band

Back Row *(Left to Right) – R Walker, W Stamp, T Clark, W Stephenson, D Plows, P Mortimer, G Eastwood* **Middle Row** *– H Wreghit, E Sutton (Snr), A Sutton, H Humphrey, W Medley, F Dawson, A Bristow, T Eastwood* **Front Row** *–D Ives, E Slater, E Sutton (Jnr),N Kilvington, L Lambeth , A Dobson, E Dobson, A Jowrey, E Jarman*

So this should have been a glorious year for the band, shouldn't it. Well it was not. The band was plagued for the entire year by really poor attendances that were very disheartening for the players who did attend regularly. There was a lack of competent cornet players and more needed to be recruited. The Learners were coming on well under Mr Lambeth's capable tutorage, but as the secretary reported at the General Meeting in January 1954, *'Our bandmaster is full of enthusiasm, but why should he have to flog a dead horse'.*

Both the chairman and the secretary berated the band for the missed opportunities of the Golden Jubilee. What had been so well anticipated, with many ambitious schemes suggested, had been marred by the disregard given to rehearsals. It was thought that much greater deeds could have been done, but they were unsupported.

The time had come for a full and frank discussion to define the next year's working policy, appoint new officials and generally pull the band together. There were harsh words in desperate times.

The actual record of the band's activities was impressive; two contests - gaining another 5th at Huddersfield and a second invitation to the Yorkshire v. Durham Contest. Unfortunately there was an insufficient numbers of players to be able to accept this invitation (again). Numerous concerts were carried out with the performances by the band being very much appreciated. Coronation Day was a wash out, but the band bravely battled on and performed their duties admirably. Two further Lunchtime concerts had been given and there would have been more if there had been sufficient players.

The Jubilee Concert was profitable but a subsequent concert planned for February 1954 had already been cancelled due to lack of players.

Mr Humphrey as ever came in for praise for the unselfish way in which he aided the chairman and gave help whenever needed.

The Bandmaster's report was short and to the point. When the officials of the band were being nominated he declined to be re-appointed as bandmaster and tendered his resignation both as a player and the bandmaster. Having been a dedicated bandmaster and enthusiastic teacher for his 9 years in office the band passed on their thanks and asked that a letter of appreciation be sent to Mr L. Lambeth.

No new bandmaster was appointed and an Assistant Bandmaster was left in abeyance until a bandmaster was appointed. In the short term it was agreed that any member could have a try at conducting the band.

Over the next 6 months the committee and Dr Macdonald made various attempts to persuade Mr Lambeth to reconsider his decision but he was immovable and who could blame him.

What a very sad end to the band's 50th year.

So the band set off into its 51st year without a conductor and dangerously short of players. Many offers of engagements were coming in and the band was accepting these, but, in view of the changed circumstances of the band at a lower rate than previously.

A letter had been received from a man offering his services as a conductor. Hitherto all the conductors had also been employees of the Works and Dr Macdonald intimated to the committee that he would like this situation to prevail if possible. With this in mind the committee wrote to Mr Laurie Bruce (conductor of the York Railway Institute Band) and asked if he might be persuaded to take the band on. Mr Bruce was fully aware of the difficulties the band had faced with poor attendances and, after some consideration, declined the offer.

Dr Macdonald suggested that the band should ask Mr Bruce to conduct one of the Lunch time concerts, perhaps if he saw the calibre of the band he might be more interested.

Meanwhile, the committee decided to try a new tactic to entice Mr Lambeth back and invited him along to meet with the committee. The committee asked him if there were any terms under which he would consider taking up the band's baton again. His reply was obviously not intended to be taken seriously. He asked for full control of the band and £40 per year. The band was unable to accept these terms. The matter was closed.

During the remainder of 1954 and into 1955 the band wrote to previous members who still worked for the firm in an endeavour to improve the numbers and several past members did rejoin. Dr Macdonald (the Labour Manager) was extremely helpful in ensuring that suitable men could get the time they needed off work to play with the band. In fact during this very period, it is difficult to see how the band could have survived without the help that Dr Macdonald gave.

Several of the band stalwarts stood firm in the face of the massive problems and with Dr Macdonald's unfailing support, they pulled the band through.

By the General Meeting in June 1955 the band still had no resident conductor (16 months after Mr L. Lambeth had resigned). The chairman referred to the difficult time the band was experiencing and thanked members for being loyal. The secretary's report normally included the lengthy list of engagements and contests that the band had completed. On this occasion it was considerably shorter. It had always been the policy of the Rowntrees Band to attend engagements with a representative band and to produce a decent standard of playing. As this condition did not exist the resultant engagements, especially important ones were reduced to a minimum with the hope that the band would come back to its own in due course.

This meeting saw the band elect Mr Harry Lawn as bandmaster for a probationary period of 3 months.

Mr Lawn had first contacted the band in August 1954 explaining that he wished to relocate to York from Surrey. He further explained that he was a cornet player and went on to expand on his musical experience and ability. He had studied music at the Royal Military School of Music, had been teaching for some time and had also been the conductor of the Crystal Palace Band for 5 years. Mr Lawn asked for the opportunity of an audition with a view to becoming a member of the cornet section.

The secretary, Mr Wreghitt had other plans for him.

Mr Lawn's letter was shown to Dr Macdonald who advised the secretary to respond confirming that Mr Lawn was looking for employment (primarily) with the works and that his interest in the band was second to this. Mr Lawn was further advised to contact Dr Macdonald directly as there were possible vacancies within the firm which he might be suitable for.

Mr Lawn, having secured an interview in September, wrote again to Mr Wreghitt advising him that he would bring along his instrument just in case the band wanted to see (hear) him. I should think the band all but bit his hand off to get him into the bandroom.

There was a lot to do, especially with the learners group which had been neglected of late and needed attention. But the really important issues seemed to be the Annual Outing and the Annual Dinner.

Mr Lawn completed his initial 3 months probationary period and was confirmed in the position and once more the band seemed to be on track. A few more applications for membership were received and a couple of players left, so the playing situation was just holding its own. However there was a steady number of attendees at rehearsals and it was obvious that the band was improving, so a couple of engagements were tentatively entered into, at Rowntree Sports and at Selby. Below is a picture taken at one of these sports days. The bandsmen always had a race.

The winners of the 1952 Bandsmens race.

One of the best engagements of this 'new beginning' was a Massed Bands Concert. The Railway Band had invited Rowntrees to take part in this during 1956. Many similar invitations had been received in the past and they had rarely been accepted. Mr Bruce and Mr Lawn set about arranging a programme.

This was also the year that the York and District Band Association was formed. A letter from Mr Bradbury was received by our committee explaining that endeavours were underway to form a Brass Band Society and asked for our assistance, along with other bands. Messrs Lawn and Dobson were nominated to represent the band at the preliminary meeting on 31st March 1956. Our Mr Dobson was elected as the first Chairman of the Association. The report from this meeting was that a committee had been elected and further meetings were planned. The subscription was to be 10/- (50p) per year. When the band was invited to vote for our membership of this society it was agreed that we should join.

The first impact of membership of the society came when the band quoted for an engagement for York Corporation. The Corporation replied that it would pay only £12 or £15 for a single or double engagement. The society had set a rate of £15 minimum for a single engagement and so the Corporation was sent our regrets, along with a short explanation of the situation. The Railway Band and the West Riding Band Association were also informed that we had rejected the Corporation fees.

Still the band needed to *'get out there and play'*. So a charity engagement at Aberford was accepted on Mr Lawn's suggestion. The chairman, in his May 1956 report to the General Meeting expressed that in his opinion *'the taking on of engagements would be an asset to the band, not only from a playing point of view, but from a social aspect. It would help to keep the band together.'* He hoped that the band would take advantage of the tuition given by Mr Lawn who was doing his best to improve the band. The Secretary added that the perennial, hampering issue was attendances at the rehearsals. Even the bandmaster said how shocked he was at the poor attendances, but in his opinion, despite being short on numbers, he felt the quality was there.

So it was agreed to advertise in the Works Magazine, to continue to contact past members and to promote two of the Learners to the band. Another Learner, who had earlier in the year lost interest, was to be contacted and, in the event that he returned, the band would pay his bus fare. It was felt that the Junior Members should have Maroon Blazers and it was agreed to go ahead and purchase these. Junior members were even given a vote, from this meeting onwards, once they reached 16. This begs the question, what age did you have to be before in order to vote?

1956 saw two more of our members receive their 50 Years Certificates. Messrs A. Dobson and H. Wreghitt had now both completed 50 years with the band. How many bands can boast that within 3 years 5 of their members (2 of whom were still playing) had received '50 Years in Banding' Certificates? Not many I am sure. These two members were also awarded Life Membership of the Brass Band Club.

Another of my favourite pieces of music was bought this year 'The Dam Busters'. Still the band only managed a few engagements this year – at Haxby, Rowntrees Sports and Selby, ending the year with two concerts in the Joseph Rowntree Theatre which made small, but helpful, profits.

The Bandmaster, February 1957 reported that he felt the band needed another 8 or 10 adult players and that this would alleviate the burden on some of the other players. He commented that he only saw some of the members at engagements and pointed out the benefits of attending rehearsals as well. He was thankful for the support he had received during the past year in pursuing his belief in playing the music of today as well as of yesterday.

Agreement was reached that representation should be made to the firm to permit us to insert an advert in the British Bandsman, worded carefully so that it did not refer to Bandsmen in particular(!). It was also suggested that all the young players were got together, before band practices, to carry out a Learners Class. The committee was to select volunteers to give the tuition and Mr Bristow intimated that he was willing to help.

At the First York and District Brass Band Association (YDBBA) Contest which took place in the Co-operative Hall, York, on 28th April, 1957, Rowntree Cocoa Works Band were awarded 2nd Prize (Hymn Tune Contest) in the 1st Section Grading. This was the first real success the band had tasted for a very long time.

The Second YDBBA Contest was held at the Railway Institute, York, on 24th November 1957. On this occasion the band struck gold (and silver). They were awarded 1st Prize in the March Contest (playing B.B. & C.F.) and also 2nd Prize in the Selection Contest (playing Indian Summer). Both of these were in the 1st Section contests.

Between these two contests however, there was another crisis that hit the band. Mr Lawn sent in his resignation and it was brought before the committee on 21st May, when after discussion it was agreed to ask Mr Lawn to withdraw it. Mr Lawn did so and the question was closed. (No, it was not that simple). It would appear that Mr Lawn had submitted a Press Report on a concert the band did in the Tempest Anderson Hall. An observation was made that Mr Lawn's report was a reference to himself and not to the general playing of the band. This had aroused dissatisfaction among the members and an extraordinary meeting was requested.

At the Extraordinary General Meeting the chairman outlined the reason for holding it. *'Mr Lawn's actions in submitting a report in connection with the park Engagement in the Tempest Anderson hall was not in accordance with the views of the members, in that no reference was made to the band's playing and only a report in the interest of himself.'* These were very harsh words. Other members reminded the meeting that this had happened before and it did not create a proper atmosphere among the members. It was understandable that these actions were such as would make the members unhappy. In his defence, Mr Lawn said he had done his best since coming to the band and was willing to step out of the breach as conductor.

Mr E.A. Sutton was then recorded as having asked Mr Lawn if he would be prepared to accept a Professional Conductor. In his opinion, and he had been a playing member since the 1920's, Mr Lawn was not up to the standard of working up a piece for a contest. This was the last straw for Mr Lawn and he tendered his resignation for the second time in four months. Mr Lawn was thanked for his services.

So who took the band to the November Contest? Well enquiries were made to Mr J. Atherton, Mr L. Lambeth and one other. By October, the committee had decided to select Mr Lambeth from the results of their enquires.

Following the contest success Mr Lambeth was once more, invited to submit his terms for taking the band. Common sense seems to have prevailed this time with terms of £15 per year being agreed with a bonus at the General Meeting if there was a sufficient surplus in the band funds.

As 1958 got underway Mr Lambeth endeavoured to get the band in order. What had happened to the Learners Group, and the Band Annual Outing and Dinner? It was obvious that he truly understood the essence of a good brass band. It required healthy competition, the opportunity to perform in public, a sound training programme for young players and a good social life. This holds as true today as it has throughout the history of brass bands.

At this General Meeting, the Chairman (Mr Dobson) who was also Chairman of the YDBBA, pointed out the functions of the Association and asked all present to take an interest in it. Mr Dobson also referred to the pleasant atmosphere which now existed since the return of Mr Lambeth. He asked members to keep together as he anticipated the band making a lot of progress. He concluded by thanking everyone for their services and support over the past year.

In his report the secretary commented on the improved attendance. He said that it was always much more interesting to play your instrument when you knew that others were making the same effort. He related the recent success at the 2 York contests to the improved attendances and felt that contests were an added incentive even though it meant hard practices.

Mr Wreghitt praised the young players in the band and said that they were acquitting themselves extremely well indeed and could become more useful players in time to come. He felt that they had played their part in the recent success the band had enjoyed in the contest arena. In addition to these contests, the two park concerts the band had fulfilled, plus one at Butlins and, of course, the annual Selby Remembrance Day, as well as the carols at New Earswick on Christmas Eve were all very well received. It was noticeable that the Museum Gardens Concert was better attended that the one in Rowntree Park. It seems that people would attend the centralized concerts more readily. Also the Museum Gardens have an alternative bad weather facility in the Tempest Anderson Hall.

Mr Lambeth added his comments to the above stating that since coming back to the band he had been surprised at the enthusiasm which existed and with the pre-contest attendance, and with these words he settled down to a further 12 years as the bandmaster.

CHAPTER 11

The welcome return of Mr Lambeth complimented the mood of the band. A more settled, ambitious and hard-working band emerged from the trials of the past two and a half years.

The band bought Premium Bonds(!), re-commenced tuition for the young players with Mr E.A. Sutton assisting Mr Lambeth and the Lunch Hour concerts were resurrected, initially with just 2 planned during the summer months. During 1958, the band enjoyed its summer Outing once more, planned another Carol Concert and said 'Happy Retirement' to Mr E.E. Sutton (the last playing member of the original 1903 band).

New uniforms were on the agenda again. The firm was prepared to give a 4 year loan of £100, plus a donation of £25, to aid the purchase, and May 1958, saw the representative from the uniform manufacturers attend the bandroom. To further enhance the bandsmen's deportment, it was agreed to purchase white shirts and bow ties.

Then there was the purchase of some mutes (6 cornet mutes plus 3 for the trombones) from Mayers and Harrison.

The band had terrific success again in the YDBBA November contest, gaining a 1st Prize in the Selection Contest (1st Section) and a 2nd Prize in the March Contest (1st Section). Whilst they did enter the Daily Herald and Belle Vue Contests, I haven't been able to find out the results.

However, below is a picture of them with the Championship Cup. This picture also features Mrs Grace Pratt the first lady to contest with the band:

roud winners of the Championship Cup at yesterday's York and District Brass Band ssociation contests in the Railway Institute gymnasium, were Rowntree's Cocoa Works Band, admiring the trophy held by Mr. L. Lambeth, their conductor.

The following year, 1959, was equally successful for the band with them taking 1st Prize in the YDBBA 'Own Choice' Selection Contest (1st Section) and 2nd Prize in the 'Own Choice' March Contest (1st Section). So the band completed an enviable 'hat-trick' at this local contest. In the age old tradition of success breeding success the band came 1st (again) in the March Contest in 1960, got a 2nd and 3rd in 1961 before returning to form in 1962 with a 1st in the Selection Contest and in 1963 they gained a 1st and 2nd in the March and Selection contests, respectively. A total of five 1st Prizes, five 2nd Prizes and a 3rd Prize out of six consecutive YDBBA Contests.

This was the most consistently successful period the band had ever had.

Here is the band photographed at the time with their winners shield and trophy in 1961:

It's terrific to be able to identify one of the present (2003) band in this picture. The young lad on the right at the front is Ken Stamp, who is now the principal trombone player. Ken's dad (W. Stamp) was recognised in 1960 for his 21 years service to the band with a £5 gift.

Mr Lambeth was presented with a Metronome in recognition of his successes with the band in the YDBBA Contests and the band members threw themselves into the contesting arena and the giving of concerts.

Naturally they also held a celebration 'social function' where the young members, under 16's, were to be given their dinner free.

One of the highlights of this period was the York Festival in 1959. This included a massed band concert, conducted by H. Mortimer, a name which even now impresses the players of today. To say that 'Harry' is a legend is to elevate the word legend to a place above and beyond its normal usage. The bands who took part in this festival included Fodens, Heltons, our band and the Railway Band. Mr Mortimer remarked how pleased he was with the playing and for the good work done by the local bands, who had apparently put plenty of practice in. He specially drew attention to the need for good attendances at practice. We all know that this is the essence of a good performance.

Apart from the previously mentioned contest success, during this period the bands calendar was punctuated by a number of interesting performances. There were further Festivals in 1960 and 1961, The Royal Wedding in 1961 when the band played in the Museum Gardens, the National Association of Brass Bands Convention (invitation only) to name but a few of the fascinating items of the bands agenda.

Mr H. Wreghitt celebrated 50 years of banding (with the same brass band) during 1962. Also, Mr L. Lambeth celebrated a 25 year connection with the band, first as a player and lately as the band master.

Both men, Harry and Les, were highly praised in the Chairman's Report (E. Dobson). He said *'It is a happy event for me this year, as we have the pleasure of showing some respect for two of the officers namely H. Wreghitt and Leslie Lambeth. In the case of our Secretary, it is no mean achievement to complete 50 years with the same band and indeed I am most pleased, happy and delighted, that I ask members to show your appreciation to Harry and also to Les (as we all know them), for their good and faithful service to Rowntree Band. I have known Harry intimately for over 50 years, and at all times he has been a bandsman in the truest sense, and for 25 years I can only say the same thing about Leslie. We should indeed be grateful that such enthusiastic bandsmen are in our midst.'* It was subsequently agreed to present both these men with the usual £5 gift.

The Secretary in his report added his thoughts for the bandsmen who had suffered illnesses through the year. He named Messrs Kilvington, Kissane and L. Bilham. Mr Wreghitt also makes special mention as follows *'we are pleased to learn that Brian Bousfield is now recovering from his recent serious illness. This was very unfortunate, as it happened on his Wedding Day. I know that you will wish, with me, that he will soon be fully restored to good health'.*

Mr Lambeth expressed some disappointment once again at the numbers of members attending rehearsals. He suggested that the quartet parties should be got together again. This would create an interest for Brian Bousfield, who unfortunately could not play, but could take charge of a group, it was thought. Mr B. Bousfield was elected assistant bandmaster along with E. Pratt at the general meeting in January 1962 in an endeavour to sustain his interest in the band following his illness.

So, in 1963 the band were celebrating 60 years in existence. The Chairman, as was customary, thanked all present at the General Meeting, and complimented the Bandmaster, Secretary and Treasurer for all the work, and the other officers for their stewardship, which at times had been difficult. Mr Dobson also asked the meeting to show their respect following the death of their old bandsman, H. Pawson, whom you may remember emigrated to Australia. Both Mr H. Pawson's sons, previous members also, have an entry in our 'Past Members' Section.

Mr Lambeth was congratulated on being invited to conduct the York Association Concert Band (massed band). His careful coaching of the juniors came in for special praise as did the effect their presence was having on the standard of the band. These young members were highly praised for their commitment to rehearsals, particularly through the severe winter months, (which saw many older members missing from rehearsals) and also for their behaviour during the rehearsals. They were considered a credit to the band as well as an obvious asset for the future of the band.

Mr Bristow, who had been the band Librarian for 43 years chose this year to step down. In appreciation of his long service to the band he was made an Honorary Member. Mr Chapman was provisionally elected as the band Librarian within a few weeks.

Two other members had reached milestones in their membership of the band: Mr L. Bilham and Mr D. Ives had both given 21 years service to the band and were granted the traditional £5 gift.

Aside from the above and the usual round of concerts and contests 1963 went past with a remarkable lack of occasion. However, for the following year, a trip was being considered. This would be to Munster, during August 1964 and would involve a combination band derived from Rowntrees and the Railway Institute. Meetings to discuss the matter were arranged between the two bands and in the end the bands did not go, on this occasion. This time they approached the city authorities with a view to extending an invitation to some of the Munster instrumentalists to come to visit York.

Contest success followed for the band as in 1963 the band gained 1st prize at Kirby Misperton Contest and 2nd Prize at Grantham contest. There were some profitable concerts given in the park and also in the Tempest Anderson Hall. There were as usual, gaps in the band and imperfections in attendances at practice.

1964 saw little Wilf Medlay retire from the band and he was made an Honorary Member. Wilf had been a dedicated member of the band, an excellent musician and had even, on occasion, been called upon as a comedian at the variety concerts which the band held in the Rowntrees Theatre.

1965 said goodbye to two further members of the band and the Secretary, at the February 1965 General Meeting said *'I would like to refer to two of our recent members of the band. First I would mention Mrs Grace Pratt, who for domestic reasons has had to discontinue her activities. Grace has rendered good service to our band and I wish to put on record our sincere thanks for the valuable help she has given during the years she has been with us. I should also like to put on record our thanks to Roy Bilham for his services. Roy appears to have dedicated himself to music making and no doubt you will want to wish him well during his army career.'*

Contest success followed the band into 1965 as, once again they took 1st Prize at the YDBBA in the March Contest and 2nd Prize in the Selection Contest. There was also a service in the Minster, which the band played at, and the conductor was, once more, Mr Harry Mortimer. This was considered a great occasion for the young players, and one which it was hoped, they would remember all their lives. Well some of them are still with the band so why don't you ask them?

The wide and varied concerts, which had become the hallmark of the band continued during this year with concerts at Alton Towers, in

Knaresborough, in the Museum Gardens (twice), the cycle Rally, the usual Hospital visits and three clubs. The only constant frustration was – you've guessed it – attendance at rehearsals… It was not possible to attend one contest (The Peoples Contest at Barnsley) due to an apparent lack of commitment by several members. At one point (7 weeks before the York Contest) the bandmaster had declared to the committee that he would resign if nothing better could be done. Following this meeting, leaflets were sent to all members informing them of the position. This seems to have done the trick and a great rally round occurred, culminating in the contest success.

The Chairman, at the 1966 General Meeting called for all the band members to work harder than their bandmaster. To him, he said, they should show their appreciation for his magnificent loyalty and patience, together with his very hard work and the service which he had given the band. Hear, hear! In recognition of his efforts the bandmaster received a grant of £5.

The bandmaster's concern seemed to lie with the influence this poor example was giving to the younger members. It was also disheartening for those who readily gave their time without fail. A very good point which sadly has reverberated around all band rooms through the ages.

This meeting also saw Mr Wreghitt, secretary for the past 20 years be elected as one of the band's Vice-Presidents. Other past members holding this position were Mr G. Lickley and Mr E.E. Sutton, with Mr A. Lickley (Jnr) being one of the three Presidents of the band.

The band name was modified at this same meeting and the band from this point forward was to be known as 'Rowntree Works Band'. The name of the band for the previous 36 years had been 'Rowntree Cocoa Works Band'. There is an appendix at the end of this book which details the names of the band through its 100 year history – only for the briefest of times has the word 'Rowntree' been absent from the name of the band.

So the newly named band embarked on 1966 with the usual issues to the fore. None of these, however, dampened the bands natural enthusiasm for contests and concerts. This year saw the disaster at Aberfan . The band organised a fund-raising concert in St George's Hall. It was however considered a financial flop. This was a joint concert with the St Lawrence Male Voice Choir and it had been well advertised, for free, in the Yorkshire Evening Press, which was leading the fund-raising events in aid of this disaster.

The week after this concert the band took 1st Prizes in both the March and the Selection Contests – maintaining their record of winning prizes on virtually every occasion that they had participated. The newly established Conductor's Prize went to Mr Lambeth – as the conductor of the band, in any section, which achieved the most points overall. Finally, Mr Lambeth gets a prize all his own.

The YDBBA held a 10th Anniversary Concert in York Minster with the Leeds Model, Rowntree's and Railway Institute bands. Mr Mortimer once again was the conductor, with our own Mr Lambeth taking some of the items.

The band Chairman, since the end of the Second World War, Mr E. Dobson, retired his Chairmanship in 1967. He was invited to join the ranks of the Vice-Presidents which he happily did. The band has always been reluctant to allow good men to simply leave. There had always been a role for past members on the committee or in an advisory capacity and once again, just when he thought he was going to be able to concentrate on retirement the band gets in the way. I have to say, it doesn't look like he put up too much of a struggle does it?

The new Chairman was Mr H. Humphrey. Mr Humphrey had been a bandsman since the late 1920's and had been the band's treasurer, assistant secretary and company liaison officer for most of the past 40 years.

Mr J. Sutton applied to rejoin the band in 1967. Johnny had been a member from 1924 until the end of WWII when he had taken more of an interest in dance bands, and formed one of his own.

Just a few months earlier the band had taken part in the Leeds Area Contest and had come 2nd in the 2nd Section. This earned them an invitation to London to take part in the National Finals. Mr Lambeth was reluctant to take on a new man into a leading position just prior to the finals, however, Mr P. Mortimer convinced the band that the priority should be to take the best band they could to London, regardless of personalities. So the band happily welcomed Johnny back. It was an all too brief return as he become ill during 1973 and died shortly after. See the chapter dedicated to the Sutton family.

Mr Humphrey wrote to the firm in 1967 on behalf on the band, putting forward our case for a set of new instruments in low pitch. He was commended by his fellow committee members for the strength of the case he put forward. Unfortunately, I can't tell you how this case was greeted, nor can I give information on how the band did in the London Finals later that year. There is a gap in the minutes now until 1976. Little is documented about this period and as such I don't wish to speculate.

There is very little documentation for the intervening years, however, there are certificates to confirm that the band (Rowntrees Cocoa Works) took part in the Harrogate and District Brass Band Association Brass Band Contest in Yeadon Town Hall on 28th October 1973. The band entered in the First Section Contests and gained 1st Prize in the Light Music Contest and 2nd Prize in the Selection Contest.

When the minutes of the band recommence on 10th September, 1976 the main thrust of this meeting is of a housekeeping nature.

There were a couple of members whose attendance and time keeping at engagements and rehearsals were well below the acceptable level. So far, it appears, verbal warnings had had no effect, so the secretary was asked to write to both of them requesting their resignation. In the event that they did not wish to resign they were to ask the committee to reconsider their case.

It was agreed that the secretary was to keep minutes of all the committee meetings and copies of all the letters on file. The bandroom required a notice board for the purpose of displaying extracts from the minutes, details of engagements and other relevant information in order to keep members up to date.

The band rules needed to be brought up to date and the details for up and coming events were thrashed out – concerts, contests, charitable events, the usual selection of activities.

Even the list of instruments was to be brought up to scratch with Mr W Stamp agreeing to do this, and to maintain it when necessary. It was decided that no instrument would be given out without the Musical Director's (MD) and 1 member of the committee's authority. In the absence of the MD then 2 committee members could authorise the issuing of an instrument. To add to the ability to keep track of instruments, a form was to be produced which bandsmen would sign acknowledging their receipt of a band instrument. Parents of younger players would be asked to sign on their behalf. A list of instruments which required repair was to be raised and estimates for the repair of them to be obtained. The most urgent seems to have been a BBb bass.

It appears as though there was a bit of a reaction from the family of one of the members who had been asked to resign, due to poor attendance and timekeeping. As a result, a member of the committee was to negotiate the situation and encourage the aggrieved member to discuss the matter with the committee. The other band member who had been sent an identical letter had not responded.

The attendance register was resurrected in an attempt to ensure that members were more easily made aware of poor attendance and fairness.

The Junior band was still functioning well with Mr Peter Mortimer as their bandmaster, and Mr Chris Lawn taking them when Mr Mortimer was working. Chris Lawn was the son of Mr Harry Lawn who had been bandmaster of the senior band in the 1950's.

By September of 1976, the wayward bandsman was still causing concern, despite having met with the committee and giving his assurance that his attendance would improve. It was felt that, due to his current domestic situation (his wife was due a baby imminently), the matter could be left over for the time being. Another month went by and the committee felt that no improvement had been seen in this member's attendance. It was then that one of the committee intervened significantly. The committee member was related to the part timer and expressed the concern that this member felt he was being singled out. It was made clear that if further action was taken against his relative then other members of the family would resign (and there were several in the band at this time). As a result further action was deferred. Hmm.

The other band member had still not replied to the secretary's letter and was still in possession of band uniforms and Mr Rochester agreed to make contact to retrieve the band uniform. There were a further two members whose attendance level had begun to raise eyebrows and the secretary was asked to write to each of them and to post details of the action against all three members on the notice board. In the end none of these players were written to at this time due to the problems of attracting new players and the illness of one of their father's.

However, the band had been advertising for new members and replies were being dealt with and contests and concerts were all in hand. So once more, it appears that the band was progressing satisfactorily. There were plans to have a march written especially for the band and the Annual Band Dinner was being organised for January 1977.

Back to the bandsman whose family ties had previously prevented him being asked to resign his membership. Well by July 1977, things had not improved. Mr Oakes, committee member, felt that the band rules should apply to everyone, pointing out another sporadic attendee. It took until November of that year for the committee to finally lose patience with this man and he was sent a letter informing him that his services were no longer required. Over a year had passed since the first occasion when the committee expressed their concern over attendance. It does seem as though this member was extended every possible opportunity to conform, and rightly had the full support – for some time – of his immediate family. However, in the end, he had to go for a while anyway.

So who was conducting the band, and who was running the band during this period? Well, Capt. Don Carson was the MD (see past members section for his personal history), the band chairman appears to have been Mr Peter Mortimer, and the other officers varied on a regular basis.

Gone it seems were the days when the secretary was in post for 40 years (or more) and the chairman likewise. The vastly experienced committees of the past had been replaced. Fewer and fewer 'company men' were now steering the band.

Rowntree's Cocoa Works was now Rowntree Mackintosh. The historians amongst you will be able to pinpoint when this occurred. I don't wish to bore the avid brass band enthusiast with company details, you would know I was making it up anyway, wouldn't you!

Capt. Carson, remained the MD until the summer of 1977 when he stepped down. Mr Ken Jackson was invited to discuss the possibility of him taking over. The band was continuing in a very unsettled period with regards to conductors. Mr Lambeth had resigned during 1969, I would love to be able to give you the details but there are none to be found. The appendix at the end of the book will show you just how unsettled this situation was. Some years show more than one conductor taking the band. We may find out why as we progress towards the present day.

The March which had been written for the band was finished. The 'RMco' was penned by Mr Derek Broadbent, a highly respected brass band composer of our times, but the march still had no name, and therefore, could not be registered with the Performing Rights Society.

This year also saw the first steps being taken by the firm to hand control of the administration of the band to the band members. The company confirmed its interest in the band and that it might be approached as and when required. The Personnel Department could still be encouraged to appoint an employee who had the potential to join the band. With regard to the advertising/public relations interest in the band, a survey was requested of other company bands e.g. John Fosters Black Dyke Mills, Hammonds Sauce Works, and many others. The board certainly wanted to assess the value of the band.

Rowntree Mackintosh had agreed to give the band a grant of £1,000 per year for three years, which the committee, initially, decided to divide as follows:

Travelling Expenses (Players)	£200
Professional Fees (Contests, Coaching, etc)	£250
Honorarium – Chairman	£ 50
Honorarium – Secretary	£ 75
Honorarium – Treasurer	£ 75
Honorarium – Librarian	£ 25
Instruments (Purchase & Repairs)	£325

The travelling expenses were further explained in the minutes. Aid with travelling expenses could be given to players who travelled to play with the band (including rehearsals) a distance greater that fifteen miles from the boundary of the City of York, at the discretion of the committee. I wonder how many players this affected.

The 2003 band has several members who travel greater than 15 miles, as well as 5 members (and the conductor) who are all travelling from West Yorkshire (in excess of 30 miles each way, per rehearsal). The 2003 band offers little financial aid to these members. Looks like this could be due to be reviewed in light of this piece of historical information.

Back to late 1977, when the band was preparing to buy a new Soprano cornet and BBb bass. They were also planning a familiar round of engagements and contests. The new conductor Mr Ken Jackson, was getting to know the band and the players. Having been asked if he would be happy for the committee to engage a professional conductor to prepare the band for contests he stated that he was against the idea, but that he would like to invite other band conductors along for their comments and suggestions regarding style etc.

It was generally agreed that the band required more personnel of a good standard, especially in the cornet section where numbers were particularly weak. It was agreed that an advertisement should be placed in the British Bandsman. Ultimately, only one reply was received as a result of this advert – A Mr T.J. Edwards who was subsequently asked to attend for audition (with the band) and interview (with the firm).

A rearrangement of the current members could benefit the band also and so it was suggested that Dennis Stamp should move to Solo Cornet, Trevor Bousfield to Flugel Horn, Ian Bousfield to Solo Trombone, Ken Stamp to Solo Horn, Edward Sutton (yes he's still playing) to 2nd Euphonium. All of these changes were agreed between the committee and the musical director and were implemented immediately. Naturally, as was the efficiency at this time, what actually happened was K. Stamp – Euphonium, D. Stamp – Solo Horn, J. Sherlock – Eb Bass, E.A. Sutton – 1st Baritone, R. Lawler – BBb Bass.

Surprisingly the band was having a problem with players who appear not to have been members just walking into the band room and sitting in with the band without the consent of the MD. It was felt that this was causing an imbalance in the band and disrupting the practices, which were so badly needed for the band to improve. It was decided that this practise must stop immediately. The MD was to enforce this decision.

However the band dinner was booked for 14th January 1978 so all was well really. As was customary, members were paid for out of band funds, but guests were to be paid for by members.

The committee was becoming increasingly anxious about the Company's commitment to them. In 1978, Mr Mortimer had written to the firm regarding the negotiations about the band's position. No reply had been received. Not even, apparently, an acknowledgement of this letter, despite an early reply being requested. One suspects that the Company had difficulties of its own to contend with. However a further meeting with the company was requested as soon as possible.

Despite his earlier reservations about the use of a professional conductor, February 1978 saw Mr Jackson agree that all would benefit from the experience and one was sought as soon as possible. Mr

Leighton Rich was engaged for the Radio Leeds Knockout Contest. The secretary was instructed to approach Mr Ken Johnson and other professional conductors to coach the band for the Area Finals.

The band had presented the company with a report conveying the costs of equipping and running a brass band worthy of carrying the name of Rowntree Mackintosh. It was pointed out that many of the instruments dated to the pre-war era and some even to the 1920's. It was stressed that many instruments would need to be replaced as a priority. This report was integrated into a statement which Mr Cordier (Personnel Manager at Rowntree Mackintosh) was submitting to the main Board. It seems that copies were sent to the band committee, but I can't find them, I'm sure it would make interesting reading.

The Annual General meeting was delayed as the committee waited for a reply from the Board.

In the meantime, the band management was divided into 3 main categories during January 1979, i.e. Personnel, Engagements and General Duties. The Personnel sub-committee were to ensure that members were aware of engagements, rehearsals and to engage deputy players, if ours were unavailable. The Engagements sub-committee were to pursue financially viable engagements (of a suitable nature) and to speed up the process of acceptance or declining of jobs. The General sub-committee were going to sort out the library, transport and social functions. Any member of the band who felt that he/she could be of assistance to any of the sub-committees was urged to make themselves available.

The minutes during May 1979 show that Mr Jackson was no longer the MD. His resignation is not listed in the minutes however, so I can't explain that one either. However Mr Rich did take the band to a contest, no results available, and they paid him £50 for this and the tuition prior to the contest. At this same meeting the resignations from 3 players were accepted and the then secretary also resigned (from the secretary's role).

So, it was back to square one, again. No conductor, few players and the committee in turmoil.

Well the acting secretary, D. Stamp, was asked to contact Mr Graham Walker (again may have been related to our earlier stalwart of a conductor in the 1930's and 40's, but, then again, maybe not), to see if he would be interested in taking over as MD. Mr Mortimer was encouraged to introduce junior members from the junior band, at his discretion.

Despite the difficulties the band were having with the loss of the guiding hands from the firm and the problems with recruitment and retention of players, it is obvious from the minutes during 1979, that the players unanimously felt that contesting should remain a high priority. There was also a move into a new band room planned and during June of this year a large number of the band accompanied Mr Durham (RM Co) to make an inaugural visit.

A number of new and returning players were auditioned during July and August and with the numbers so boosted the Chairman proposed a series of concerts to provide sufficient funds to keep the band going. The secretary was asked to approach various clubs and organisations for engagements. As the year progressed, the band was still without a MD. However several new members had joined and a number of significantly well paid engagements had been secured. Some adverts for players (employees) were to be placed in the Merthyr Times, the Glasgow Herald and the Sunderland Echo. It was also agreed that the secretary should approach the university regarding placing adverts there for potential players. Finally, some pamphlets had now been agreed and were soon to be printed and distributed.

At the Annual General Meeting, 2nd December 1979 the elected committee is finally identified. The Chairman (as suspected) is Peter Mortimer, Secretary – Trevor Collins, Treasurer – N. Robinson, Contesting Secretary – Ray Rochester, Transport – David Oakes. The band also welcomed two more new players who had been 'fixed up' with accommodation and jobs, making eight new or returning members in the second half of the year. A fine end to a very weak and insecure year.

CHAPTER 13

Here we are, a new decade, and a much more settled start to 1980 than the band had seen over the previous four years. A new bandmaster was appointed in March - David Wood. One of the members who had departed for the Railway Band during 1979 wanted to return to the RM Band and the committee invited him to submit a written application.

The band was, for the second time in its history, contemplating making a record. Discussions were taking place with EMI and their representative was to call into the bandroom for further discussion. The band was still widely publicising its need for more players, this time in Lincoln, Belfast and Birmingham, and a further three enquiries had been received, including one applicant from Ireland whose return train fare and one night's accommodation was to be paid by the band!

Engagements were being carried out regularly including the Lord Mayors Parade, one at the Cheshire Home, some in the Museum Gardens and at the Racecourse. The band dinner, as always, was being organised, this time in Elliott's on 9th February. Two guests were invited along, Mr G. Whitham and Mr A. Durham. The 2003 band are very familiar with Mr Geoff Whitham as he has coached and conducted us on several occasions since the appointment of our present bandmaster, Mr William Rushworth. Geoff is held in the highest regard by the current band and it must have been so in 1980, why else would he have been invited along.

Mr Arnold Durham was the Rowntree Mackintosh manager with whom the band had most contact during this period. He was still a great friend to the band right into the 1990's when he retired. There is a great sense of continuity developing here once more. With the band having been through the most unsettled episode of its existence it is reassuring to note that of the friends and members associated with it during 1980 many still have a favourable association in 2003.

The new bandmaster was in post and he proposed that a questionnaire be given to each member to be completed (voluntarily). This would enlighten Mr Wood as to the strengths and weaknesses of each player. He then planned to present each player with a reply showing the areas in which practice would be beneficial.

I knew it was too good to be true when, in October 1977, the committee sanctioned expenses for players travelling more that 15 miles outside the city boundaries (including rehearsals). The meeting which was held on 11th May 1980 sought to change the position by stating that expenses would only be paid for extra rehearsals and engagements, not on practice nights, if the player has to travel more than 15 miles from the boundary of York. Confused? I am, as there is no amendment shown in the minutes to back up this change of heart. Oh well, back to the drawing board.

The possibility of the band touring came up a few times in the early months of 1980. The first suggestion was for a relatively simple tour of Scotland. The second however was for a more elaborate tour of France.

Here is another charming insight into the workings of a bandsman's mind. September 1980 saw the bandmaster approach the committee looking for clarification of the current rules regarding membership. The reply was this: '... *in accordance with current rules (Rule 5), membership is permitted only with the approval of the elected committee. In the recent past, several members have resigned and joined other bands. In some cases it is apparent that temporary resignation has been used with the aim of disrupting the stability and progress of the band, OR as a weapon to assert a point of view. The committee is aware of the situation and finds it unacceptable. Should any ex-member re-apply for membership, then the committee will, as a matter of current policy, only consider re-applications after discussion with the band conductor.'* That's pretty clear now, isn't it? It's sad to think that any bandsman or woman would seek to manipulate a band in this way and still wish to be accepted as a member.

The band was in deep negotiations with the company on a number of issues. The first topic was the band room. Renovations and alterations needed to be carried out and these had been approved by the Board. The needs of the band were not terribly high on the company's list of priorities and so this situation was crawling along. Mr Arnold had also been approached for funding to record the band. He had agreed to seek donations from a variety of sections within the company, but, as the year drew on, nothing had come of this issue. A letter had also been drafted to the company asking if the band could repay their outstanding monies and then borrow some more capital in order to purchase a new set of uniforms. The reply to this was keenly awaited.

Mr Mortimer was still doing an outstanding job with the Junior Band as well as being the band Chairman but by November of 1980 he was in need of assistance and the matter was discussed by the committee. It was pointed out that there were few qualified to assist. Peter elaborated on the help needed, explaining that the required help was more along the lines of a few senior members sitting with the juniors to help them follow the music. The formation of parent's group was also discussed and it was agreed to send a circular to the parents of the junior band to determine the level of support that might be given to such a group.

Mr Mortimer wanted to concentrate on the Junior Band, and so at the Annual General Meeting in March 1981 he thanked the committee for supporting him over the past year. He also thanked the bandmaster, Mr D. Wood. Peter felt that we should continue to give all the encouragement we could to the young of the band and stated that he would prefer to stand down as chairman and run the Junior Band.

In the Bandmaster's Report Mr. Wood opened by thanking the whole of the band for the support and work put in for the recent contests. It was his opinion that the Vaux Contest was the band's best result to date (sorry, I don't know what this result was). Mr Wood emphasised that the band must not sit back, but work even harder for Belle Vue. He wanted sectional practices to commence immediately and in closing said that he felt we should all try to attract as many new members as possible, especially experienced players.

The secretary complained that there was still insufficient help from all members when moving the band instruments, music and stands. This remark was aimed at engagements and practices. Most of the AGM reports through the century echo these comments. With the possible exception of attendances at rehearsal, this has always been the single most regular complaint which committees have expressed to the band.

Mr Wood, who had only been bandmaster for slightly over a year resigned during June 1981. Again his reasons were not minuted and I can find no trace of his letter amongst the archives, so I cannot elaborate on his reasons. The band decided to approach Capt. Phillip Evans to offer him the position of Musical Director and Mr Trevor Bousfield was to be approached by the chairman to offer him the bandmaster's post.

Both of these appointments were accepted and the band direction was discussed at length during the committee meeting of September 1981. The new bandmaster brought up a number of points for further discussion. In his opinion, the forward planning was not good enough.

Regrettably, it was accepted that until a full commitment by the whole band was received it would be impossible for the committee to plan ahead. They hoped that with a new bandmaster, the commitment from the band would improve.

Mr Bousfield wanted notice boards to display band positions and engagements. This he was assured was already in hand and would be happening soon. He also felt that greater communication on the selection of music, between the MD and bandmaster had been an issue in the past and hoped that with two new postholders this problem would rectify itself.

Finally Mr Bousfield wanted better communication between band and committee. It was agreed to fix committee meetings to the first Monday of each month, thus allowing members to raise points with committee members, for discussion at meetings. Once the new notice boards were erected, the members should then be made aware more easily of events and the secretary was asked to display the minutes of meetings on these boards.

The band was saddened by the news of the death of Mr J. Stirk. As 'no flowers' had been requested by his family, the committee agreed to send the value of a wreath to 'Kidney Research'. Again, I would love to be able to tell you more about this man, but the records don't hold any more information. Suffice to say that he must have been liked and respected by the band for them to offer this donation.

Storm clouds were gathering between the company and the band. It seems that the bandsmen had dropped the practise of annual subscriptions. Ever since the band's formation, annual subscriptions had been required from its members. The company appears to have discovered that this had ceased and was anxious to ensure it was reinstated. They are reported as having stated '*if support (from the company) is to continue, the band must return to subscriptions*'. After some discussion, the figure of £10 per annum was agreed. This was to include a band jersey. Junior members would pay £5 but would have to purchase their own jersey.

There were the usual issues surrounding the repair of instruments and which players should change positions to aid the makeup of the band. The new MD offered to invite a second percussionist along, from the army, as the band had only one presently. He wished further approaches to be made to a number of players who were not currently members of Rowntree Mackintosh Band He also stated that he would discuss further player moves with the chairman to establish if such moves would be welcomed by the individual members.

Finally, he stated that the band, in order to continue to improve needed to find as soon as possible, a flugel, Soprano, 1st Baritone and Solo Cornet players. Not bad, that's only 4 key positions to fill, what an improvement on 1976.

New uniforms were back on the agenda. This seems to come up every ten years or so. Also the committee were looking into the possibility of purchasing sweaters and the trip to France was still on the table, but progress was painfully slow.

So the November 1981 General Meeting got underway with the largest number in attendance (26) that I've noted at any point in the band's history.

The chairman made the predicable 'could do better' statements as did the secretary. The new MD (Phillip Evans) opened his remarks with thanks for the support and the welcome given to him. He felt that it would take approximately two years for the band to reach the required level (but he doesn't expand on what the required level is). Some more positional changes were needed he said, in addition to the ones which had already been made. A minimum of seven players were needed (oh dear, that figure has increased again) and they needed to be experienced players. Capt. Evans stated that the band must have two hour rehearsals and that they must start on time. By pulling together now, he felt that we would get back into the prizes and thereby attract more players. With regards to contesting, he proposed that the band work for a year, bringing the standard of play up before entering another contest. Finally he encouraged more senior players to help with the Junior Band.

The newly appointed bandmaster (Mr Bousfield) continued with this theme, remarking that the band was clearly lower second section standard and would remain so, despite the wonderful work done by Phillip with existing players. Even with a greater individual input from those existing players he felt that the band would not rise to the top of the second section. Mr Bousfield identified what he considered to be the issues requiring immediate attention as the acquisition of both a Principal Cornet and Solo Horn player. Advertising in the British Bandsman was proposed.

In spite of Capt. Evans recommendation that the band not contest for the next year, the following committee meeting (only two weeks later) saw them proposing entry into two contests (Bradford Area and Belle Vue). It's does not surprise me therefore, that there is no record of the band's achievements at these contests.

However, Mr Mortimer did get help with the Junior Band following his appeal at the AGM. Mr D. Kirby agreed to act as JB Deputy Bandmaster (to liaise with Mr Mortimer), and Mrs Sue Bowater accepted the position of Junior Band Administrator. Mrs Bowater had just become the first woman ever to serve on the band committee, having become a non-playing committee member at the earlier AGM.

By January 1982, Mrs Bowater was acting Chair(man) of the band, following Mr Mortimer's resignation from the band. Mr Mortimer had tried for the past two years to be un-elected as chairman and, as was their way, the band wouldn't let a good man go. His resignation was accepted reluctantly but unanimously and the band President (Mr K. Dixon, Rowntree Mackintosh) was written to asking him to make a presentation to Mr Mortimer at the next band dinner. It was proposed that Mr Kirby be asked if he would take over as bandmaster of the Junior Band.

Mr Kirby accepted the post of JB bandmaster and requested that, in future, he would like it referred to as the Rowntree Mackintosh Youth Band. He was also keen to write to the parents of the Youth Band with a list of future engagements and ask them to consider whether a change in practice night could be considered. Furthermore, he proposed personally approaching headmasters of all local schools for Youth Band recruits. He comes over as a very enthusiastic man, so much so, that he was also elected as Deputy bandmaster for the Senior band.

The band were also concerned about becoming too dependent on the Army members and were keen to train a suitable member of the band as a conductor to avert a possible crisis in the future.

The Senior Band were busy discussing the difficulties it faced if they were to enter the Area Contest. It was felt however that the Band should participate. The MD then produced a list of proposed rehearsals that would be required and agreed to announce these at the next practice, and to produce sufficient copies for all band members and one for the Notice Board.

The Band Dinner was also being planned, and for the first time, all members were to pay for themselves as well as for guests. On the previous occasion there was difficulty meeting the cost of the dinner as the band was having financial difficulties. This year the charges would be £6 for adults (members or not) and £3 for youths who were still at school.

At the meeting in March 1982 it was announced that the band was making great progress administratively. The VAT situation, which was the band's responsibility now, was in hand, the books were now being kept up to RM standards and contests and concerts were being planned. Also being planned was the purchase of jumpers (sweaters) for the players and also a trip to Germany. The Area Contest was approaching and all seemed well. So what happened? Yet another gap in the band minutes, this time only a few months, but never the less a lot happens in a few months. Obviously, I have spoken to members of the band who were also members of the band at this time, but I am reluctant to put on record different view points none of which will expose the whole picture. So, with your permission, once again we will make a small leap forward in time and continue our story in January 1983.

Just before we go ahead and do that, I would like to mention that 1982 also saw Mr. W Stamp celebrating 45 years service with the band. Whilst presentations had not previously been given for 45 years service it was felt appropriate that he should receive a presentation at this time. Mrs Bowater agreed to purchase a suitable present. Mr Stamp had introduced all of his children to the world of banding. Ken (now Solo Trombone), Dennis (now 1st Horn) Ray and Pauline (now both retired from the Band). They were humorously known as 'The Stamp Collection'.

CHAPTER 14

So here we are in 1983. Let's try to pick up the threads of the band story. Mrs Bowater, Mr Collins, Mr Kirby, Mr Overton and Mr Robinson are no longer on the committee. The current committee, after an un-minuted AGM are Ray Rochester (in the Chair), Elizabeth Rochester (Treasurer), Eva Moorhouse (Secretary), Bob Garrity (Musical Director), Peter Mortimer (yes, he's back) and John Coates.

The new committee were discussing a trip to Germany (I'm not sure if this is the same one as before, or a second one); purchasing sweaters, getting all the uniforms in for inspection and cleaning and (can you guess what else…?) advertising for more players, especially trombones and basses.

The band trip to Germany was cancelled within the early months of 1983. It seems that the band we were 'exchanging' with was fully booked during the period which had been proposed. Another trip was swiftly organised, this time to Dijon in France. This trip had been proposed in 1980 but now it seems it was going to take place. The Dijon Council had suggested dates of 10th to 18th September (inclusive) and that this would reduce the cost to the band by 50%. With typical Yorkshire shrewdness this opportunity was accepted enthusiastically.

Overseas trips are very expensive and complicated to organise. The first item on the agenda for such a trip must be insurance. When an entire band set of instruments is being ferried or flown abroad the worst scenario must be that any of the instruments could be damaged or lost. The first quote the band received for insurance on this trip detailed that the minimum claim was £1,000. The committee considered this to be a ridiculous figure and a meeting was requested with Mr Durham, RM.

The band had a new Principal Cornet player in Edmond (Eddie) Hallow and had agreed to purchase a new, large bore, sovereign cornet for him. A few of the players were being moved around again and there was a steady trickle of players applying to join, or, as was the case for the Overton family (father and both sons) rejoining. I hesitate to say that things are coming together again.

There was also a steady number of engagements coming in, at Linton-on-Ouse, the British Legion (Tadcaster) etc. The Junior Band was resurrected, on Fridays between 7 and 8 pm and letters were being sent out to various councils and venues to try to get some summer engagements for the band.

Financially the band was in a bad way. In March 1983 plans were underway to sell off the oldest instruments in order to raise some cash. For sale were a Sovereign Euphonium, a flugel and a trombone. It was also felt necessary to raise the subscriptions to £15 per year, a suggestion which was rejected by the members at the AGM. Those wonderful expenses were under review as well. Now all expenses had to go before the committee for approval.

It seems that the new MD was having difficulties attending rehearsals and so the number of rehearsals and engagements he attended dictated his fee. Shortly after this he resigned due to pressure of work, not the money situation. Mr Mortimer was active in approaching potential candidates to replace him. David Wood was one of those asked. Remember him, conductor just a few years earlier. Mr Wood's fee, at £25 per rehearsal was too high for the band though, in the present financial predicament, the committee had offered £15. In the short term Peter Mortimer was acting bandmaster. He requested that this situation be reviewed monthly.

By June 1983 Mr T. Bousfield was back at the front of the band. One of his conditions of returning to the band was to be given full control and not to act as 'dogsbody'. Discipline in the bandroom needed to be tightened, players were to warm up prior to the rehearsal starting and there was to be no smoking during a rehearsal. Players were (once again) being shuffled around the band and a register was being put on the notice board to check that players earned their places, by coming to rehearsals. It was hoped that the trip to France would encourage membership.

In October 1983 it was recorded in the minutes that five members of the band had gone across to Dijon (5th to 10th September) on a 'fact-finding' trip. They had met with the Dijon York Association and also Mr Mariller, President of Des Trompettes Dijonnaises. This meeting was held in the bandroom of Des Trompettes Dijonnaises who were keen on the idea of 'twinning' and wanted RMB to join in their wine festival during 1984. To further this, requests for financial aid were made to both bands.

The AGM held on 27th February 1984 shows the Chairman, Ray

Rochester, recapping on the position the band is in. He said that the past year had been very difficult due to such problems as losing members and conductors. However Trevor Bousfield was appointed MD in July 1983 and preparations were well underway for the forthcoming trip to Dijon. There was a great deal of 'behind the scenes' work being dealt with by the chairman, treasurer and Brian Heskin.

New uniforms were being considered by the company and definite details and information would be available in the near future. The chairman felt that the year had ended on a very encouraging note, following the Radio York Contest. Although the result was not in our favour, satisfaction was gained by giving a fine performance and probably more important was the fact that other competing bands and radio listeners were given quite a surprise by the quality of our performance.

The bandmaster, in his report said that his return to the band had been during a very low period in the band's performance and membership. Some of the band's problems he had been aware of when he accepted the post but there were others that showed themselves sometime later. Since then, he continued, the general standard of the band had improved and a number of problems had been resolved. In his opinion though, the band was still dangerously close to disaster when *'individual considerations take precedence over those of the band'*.

Solving the remaining problems would not be easy, as the steady decline of the band had been over many years and the bandmaster expected a degree of patience in this matter. A major disappointment to him had been the disgraceful attendance at the special sectional rehearsals held for the York contest.

The bandmaster had expectations of the players. Once an engagement had been democratically accepted, then that should be considered a contract of employment and that any member of the band who finds he cannot attend should arrange for a deputy to take his place. A great idea, in theory, but I have my doubts that it would succeed in practise.

Discipline was still an issue. The bandmaster considered that in the case of a few members, their playing discipline would improve immediately if they improved their personal discipline in the bandroom. Finally, he wanted to see an extension to the band members regarding the decision making process and the general organisation of the band and wanted to see more people prepared to accept this new responsibility. *'Do something about it, for in the last analysis you get the band you deserve.'* Strong words indeed, let's see what effect they had.

Where better to find out how the year developed than to get right to the following year's AGM report. Monday 19th November 1984, (yes, two AGM's in one year, that's a contradiction, I know, but I wasn't a member then).

The chairman reported that the year had been one of progress. The company had started to take an interest in the band again and had increased their annual grant from £2,400 to £3,000. The band had received more publicity and press coverage and had also been seen more by the public and he had no doubts that the company was getting value for money.

The high point of 1984 was, quite obviously, the trip to Dijon. The band had the honour of leading the parade for the Annual Wine Festival through the city, see the photograph below, courtesy of Trevor Collins:

The band had also had some contest success in progressing through to the Final of the year's Radio York Contest (still to take place at this point).

Mr G.E. Pratt (Ted), was to re-acquaint himself with the band. With effect from 1st January 1985, he had been appointed bandmaster of the Junior Band (later renamed the Training Band). Here is a picture of Ted, courtesy of his widow, Mrs Grace Pratt:

This is how most people will remember Ted, smiling all the time. A talented, dedicated musician, a loving husband, father and grandpa, an all round nice man.

The band said goodbye to two transient members of the band. Both Mr Jones' would be returning to Australia after their year's stay in York. They were very reassuring at previous AGM's by remarking that the difficulties the band had with attendances etc., were worldwide issues that bands had always faced, and continue so to do.

There were sixteen members of the band who had left during 1984 – that's almost two-thirds of the band, but they had gained eight new members – you do the maths. This must have been a baptism by fire for the new secretary, a horrendous introduction to the workings of the National registry. The new secretary also discovered that the band had not been entered for the Regional Qualifying Contest (Yorkshire). At the eleventh hour, however, Herculean efforts enabled the band to enter the Northern Area. Coincidentally, this happened when the area boundaries were changing. For the band this was a fortunate coincidence.

Despite the huge changes in personnel within these ten months, the bandmaster felt the playing standard of the band had improved and that concert performances reflected this, as did the contest results (sorry, still don't have these in the archives, be patient – there are more to come).

Sounds once again as though the band had settled and could build on this position and improve on it. However, things are just not that simple in this band and 1985 saw huge turmoil for the umpteenth time in these past ten to fifteen years.

January 1985 started calmly enough, tracking down instruments and uniforms from all those departed players. An inventory was carried out, not only to re-establish where the instruments were, but also to assess the condition they were in. The only hint that something might be going awry was the sudden resignation of the secretary. Also, the company had approached the committee and invited them to a meeting later in the month. The company wanted the band to perform on 29th April, and when the committee expressed doubt, the band's commitment to the company was questioned. The company were interested to know if the band would consider playing at their other factories in the UK, and Europe (including Ireland). I would imagine the committee felt that the band was in no shape to play anywhere currently.

This didn't slow the band down from making plans for a further visit to Dijon!

The company also had audited the financial records of the band. In fact, the company had them from October 1984 until March 1985. When they were finally returned, a letter suggesting that a change of treasurer would be advisable accompanied them. It seems that the bookkeeping had become more and more complicated over the past few years and a simpler method of bookkeeping should be adopted.

A new treasurer was elected and the previous treasurer handed over all the accounts to the chairman, in a new black leather briefcase. The chairman, in turn, handed over the briefcase and contents to the new treasurer. It is significant that they were in this briefcase, as it became the source of some rancour over the course of the following few months. By May 1985 the accounts were being kept in a cardboard box, and so the previous treasurer asked for the unused briefcase to be returned to him.

Incidentally, there was no suggestion that there had been any false accounting by the treasurer, only that the accounts were not as simple as they might be. A band member had carried out an independent audit of the accounts and reported to the committee that they were very detailed and up to date. However the briefcase does appear to have gone missing. In the event, the chairman and the new treasurer were unable to explain, to the satisfaction of the committee where it was. Shortly thereafter, the company received notice of their decision to resign from both the committee and the band. Despite several attempts to confirm this with them directly, the two persons involved never informed the committee of their departure.

Moving on, the year 1985 was turning out to be a really interesting one. Two special events were planned, one for August and one in September. The August event was remarkable on more than one level. HMS York (the new one) was being commissioned at Rosyth (Scotland) on 9th August and the band was invited to accompany the Blessing, on the dockside, in the naval base. I have been told that this was (and maybe still is) the only occasion when a civilian band has been granted such an honour.

Below is an informal photograph of the band on this special occasion:

Amongst the items presented to the band was a beautiful painting of the ship, a plaque and a plate. Not all of these items are still in the possession of the band sadly. On the opposite page is a reproduction of the painting the band was given:

I am sure you will agree that this is a beautiful reminder of a fantastic day in the life of the band. One of the current members vividly remembers the details of this trip and I have chosen to let him tell the story. You will find it in the Senior Band 'Behind the Stand' section towards the end of the book.

Not satisfied with one terrific event during the year, September was another great event. The Rowntree Theatre was celebrating its 50 years anniversary, and chose both the Senior Band and the Junior Band to perform at the celebration concerts (Seniors did two dates and the Juniors did one).

On the following page is an extract from the original programme.

THE ROWNTREE MACKINTOSH BAND
SENIOR PLAYERS - 20th & 22nd
MUSICAL DIRECTOR TREVOR BOUSFIELD

TRIUMPHAL FANFARE	**ELGAR**
RHAPSODY ON NEGRO SPIRITUALS	**ERIC BALL**
RUSALKA'S SONG TO THE MOON	**A. DVOŘÁK**
ARRANGED BY GORDON LANGFORD SOLOIST MANDY ROBINSON	
FLY ME TO THE MOON	**BART HOWARD**
ARRANGED BY TREVOR BOUSFIELD	
MARCH – MONARCH	**W. RIMMER**

CORNET	CORNET	EUPHONIUM	TROMBONE
MANDY ROBINSON	DAVID BANCROFT	DAVID OAKES	JULIET BEECH
DAVID ROBINSON	PAUL KIND	JONATHAN WOOD	RICHARD COOPER
JOHN MILSON	LISA SHAW	RICHARD CLARKSON	**BASS**
DAVID BLACKBURN	**TENOR HORN**	**BARITONE**	DAVID WATKIN
PAULA BANKS	DAVID COPLEY	JULIE CLARK	MARTIN OVERTON
ROSALIND BINGLE	DERIC LOWE	EDWARD SUTTON	TREVOR COLLINS
MARK SHAW	TRACY SMITH	**TROMBONE**	PATRICK HUNTER
CLIFF CUNNINGHAM	**FLUGEL HORN**	KEITH MORTON	**PERCUSSION**
FRANK DAWSON	JANE CUNNINGHAM	ANDREW POMFRETT	NORMAN ROBINSON

JUNIOR PLAYERS - 21st
MUSICAL DIRECTOR TED PRATT   CONDUCTOR MICHAEL PRATT

MARCH VERMONT	**E. SIEBERT**
VALSE MONTANA MOONLIGHT	**E. SIEBERT**
BAREBACK RIDERS	**STUART JOHNSON**
FROM THE CIRCUS SUITE	
THE OLD RUGGED CROSS	**BENNARD**
SOLOIST SARAH GLOVER	
PINK PANTHER THEME	**HENRY MANCINI**

CORNET		TENOR HORN	BARITONE
DAVID BLACKBURN	SAM KIND	JANET WILSON	KATE ELLIS
SHAUN MEEK	STEPHEN WALSH	CHRIS BURGIN	MARTIN STOKES
SARAH GLOVER	KATHRYN DALE	PETER RAWCLIFFE	**BASS**
LEE DURRANT	REBECCA TODD	JULIE HARRISON	DAVID WATKINS
TIM HOLMES	SIMON DONNELLY	**EUPHONIUM**	DAVID FOX
SALLY BIRCH	RUPERT GREGORY	PETER MIDDLETON	**DRUMS**
PETA BULMER	SOLOMAN BURT		CHRIS SYKES
	JONATHAN SYKES		

If you look closely, you will see the names of two members of the 2003 Senior Band. In the 1985 Senior Band there is Paul Kind and in the 1985 Junior Band is Sally Birch. Please also notice our dear old friend, Ted Sutton, still playing with the band. Take a look also at the name of the conductor of the Junior Band. Yes, it is our own Mike Pratt, now happily playing Euphonium with the 2003 Senior band, although I'm not sure he wouldn't rather be waving the baton, even now.

Along the way there had been a return visit from the Dijon Band which barely merits a mention in the minutes. A bit hard to compete with the other highlights of the year perhaps. Finally, this year, the Annual Dinner was being planned for January 1986 at the Pike Hills Golf Club.

The round up to the year was the AGM, in November 1985. Many references were made to the events, good and bad that had punctuated the year, but the bandmaster felt that *'if these problems continue to be approached in a democratic way, and most importantly, in a spirit of friendly co-operation, then there should be no reason why the band should not continue to progress'*. With regard to the contests (no results to give yet), he reported *'the results have reflected the best that you can do, or to be more precise, the best that you are prepared to do.'*

1986 was a much calmer year compared with 1985. The band put its head down and its stands up and concentrated. Two contests were entered and lots of engagements were carried out, particularly at RAF Linton-on-Ouse, where the band did a total of 8 concerts for a variety of evening events in the Officers' Mess. The band organised a barbecue and invited the newly appointed band President, The Lord Mayor of York. There was between 80 and 90 people at the event, quite a barbecue.

The Junior Band was being asked to carry out engagements. So far nothing had been asked of the juniors, only to turn up to practice and get good enough to join the seniors. It was felt that the time had come for them to start earning their keep! It cost the Senior Band £500 per year to provide a conductor for the Juniors, plus all the music and instruments, now it was pay back time it seems. It was also felt that preparing for a performance would add some excitement to their rehearsals, perhaps even a sense of urgency and that the experience would be beneficial for the young players. What happened next is not fully explained in the minutes – Mr H. Bousfield took over as conductor of the Junior Band (?) – not for long, but no reason is given at the time.

Great excitement – I have a contest result for you – 1986, Peterlee Contest – the band got a cup for winning 1st Prize – hurrah.

CHAPTER 15

What could 1987 have in store for the band. Recent events might suggest that a rocky road lay ahead or perhaps we were entering a more settled period in the band history. Let's see.

Well the bandmaster, Mr Bousfield left early in the year, and Mr Duncan Beckley joined the band as bandmaster towards the end of the year. Not a sound basis for stability.

However, the band did excel in the thoughtful stakes. They decided, unanimously to ask Mr E.A. Sutton (Ted), to be the President of the band, along with the Lord Mayor. Now that was nice. What a great reward for his many years membership. Ted was always a dedicated player and frequently a committeeman but for the past twenty years or more he had been the librarian. With the exception of a short spell away in the services during the Second World War, Ted had been a stalwart of the band since 1921, an amazing 66 years, and he was still a playing member.

There were contests too and results. In the Area Contest (3rd Section) the band came a lowly 7th, but later in the year gained 4th place at Skegness Contest. The best result of the year came in Rossington Contest where they were awarded 1st Prize. No result is available for the Nostell Priory Contest.

The band also held another barbecue. These were beginning to replace the Annual Dinner. Some other social events were organised and once again a trip was suggested. This time the trip, planned for 1988, was to be to Holland. As it turns out, the band went to Renfrew (Scotland) instead. Exchange trips were arranged between Rowntree Mackintosh Band and Renfrew Burgh Band.

This gives me the chance for a little indulgence, as Renfrew Burgh Band was the band I played for prior to starting my own family, and my sister, Irene was (and still is) a playing member there. When Renfrew Burgh Band did the return visit to York, I went to watch the concert in the Rowntree Theatre with my husband. This was the first time I had heard Rowntree Mackintosh Band. I'd love to say that this was what rekindled my interest in banding, but I was still too busy being a mum to be able to give the necessary commitment.

Enough of this, back to the band and forward into 1988 (there really wasn't much else going on in 1987).

This was the year when the Solo Contest (now renamed the Slow Melody Contest)was resurrected. In the past, these had been an important part of the band year, and there had been quartet contests which were equally as popular. In this instance there was good reason for reinstating this contest. It was suggested that this might be a way of getting the Junior members more involved. The contest was to be held one week before the Annual Band Dinner and the prizes would be awarded on the evening of the dinner.

What an interesting year this was turning out to be. The band gained 1st Prize in the North of England Area Finals (3rd Section) and were on the way to London for the Finals. Here is a picture of bandmaster, Duncan Beckley, with the Winners Trophy (Chairman Trevor Collins is on the right):

They look pleased with themselves, don't they.

Frustratingly, just as things are going so well, there is another break in the minutes and I can't tell you what happened for the rest of the year. Yes, there were lots of engagements, we know that from the AGM in November 1988. We know that the retiring secretary, K. Morton, was anxious about how the band was behaving with regards the conductor. In fact, I've extracted some of his comments for you to peruse. He said *'that this year had been a great success in both contesting and engagements, that would show on the balance sheet.'* The band had fulfilled 26 engagements and attended 4 contests. Mr Morton added that *'he would like to thank all the members who gave up their time and expense to attend the 'Hands off Rowntrees' campaign'*. However, all didn't go smoothly and he complained bitterly about the support given for many of the engagements. The worst was at the Race Course when only eight of our members attended and at total of 46 deputy players had had to be found over the course of the year – and that's a lot of money.

Mr Beckley had brought a lot of changes to the band. Ten members left and ten new ones replaced them. He maintained that no member had been 'sacked' due to their playing ability, only due to their lack of commitment and he planned to continue to look into the problem of commitment.

The secretary continued with *'some members say that since Duncan has been conducting, the band has deteriorated socially, and they are not happy with rehearsal changes, and feel insecure with the outgoing and incoming personnel.'* He suggested that it was up to the band to decide if they wanted a happy, socialising band or a successful one. In my opinion, this doesn't have to be an either or situation. The 2003 band has a good balance between the social side of banding, well received concerts and contest success. It seems to be down to the attitude displayed within the bandroom. A serious rehearsal, contest or concert does not exclude a pleasant social gathering afterwards.

In the wake of coming 1st in the 1988 Area Contest, the band was not in a position to enter the 1989 Areas. Why? Well, more dissent within the band and some unpleasantness between the committee, the conductor and the band members. The details are not altogether clear from the records, however, it seems that the issue began over the telephone order of, and subsequent purchase of an Eb Bass.

It appears that a BBb Bass was needed and in error, the conductor ordered an Eb. The committee met and ultimately agreed to purchase the Eb anyway. The BBb which was needed was eventually bought as well. But this was just the beginning of the problems. The conductor had been employed by another band, in the same area and section as Rowntree Mackintosh. The question regarding his commitment to RM had to be asked and an unsatisfactory response was given. It was felt better at this point, by the committee, to let the conductor go to concentrate on the other band. In other words, on 1st March 1989 he was sacked. There is, as always, much more to the story than just this little snippet, but in the interest of not offending those who are still alert enough to sue me, I'm not going into any more detail. In any case, there doesn't appear to have been any animosity over this and each wished the other well.

However, the band was furious at not being kept informed of what the committee had been 'planning'. A transcript of the extraordinary general meeting that followed illustrates how disappointed the band was with the committee's decision. In the interests of fairness (and anonymity) I will paraphrase the meeting. The chairman explained that eleven band members had requested the meeting. These members had all signed a letter and sent it to the committee. The purpose of the meeting was to air all the views of the band, and not necessarily about the out-going conductor. It became clear that this was the only issue the members wished to discuss.

There was a general feeling that the actions of the committee had been planned in advance and the conductor had not been given sufficient notice of their discontent. This was hotly disputed by the Chairman, who reflected that the build up of circumstances had caused this action to be taken and that much thought and consideration had been given, on the night, before ultimately agreeing that this was the only course of action open to the committee.

The chairman alluded to the naivety of the committee in not seeing earlier that the conductor was managing the committee when the reverse should have been the case. He also reflected on the ease with which hindsight can be applied to a situation and a better solution is often found by those not directly involved. It was deemed difficult to explain to the band what the problems were leading up to this situation, as the conductor was always there.

Moving on, the band appointed T. Walmsley on a temporary contract and planned for him to take them to the Area Contest, but in the event too many players were lost over the above issue to make it possible for the band to compete. So the hunt was on for a new, permanent conductor, one who could unite the band and build on the previous year's success.

During April 1989 however, the band were approached by the City of York Council to play at a very special engagement. The newly completed Coppergate Centre was to be visited by HRH Prince

Charles, the Prince of Wales. Please find below an informal photograph of the event, kindly supply by Mr Frank Dawson:

Despite the excitement of this unique performance, the band still had huge problems. It took all of the rest of this year to pull the band round. The finances were a mess, they had debts to the company, to instrument suppliers and to uniform manufacturers, but they worked hard. An enormous number of engagements were fulfilled, most of them without a full band present. Local deputy players were paid a flat rate of £5 and players from further afield had to negotiate their 'expenses'. The instrument list was in disarray, as was the uniform list and instruments, in particular a bass trombone, were missing.

Mr Durham, Rowntree Mackintosh, was instrumental in supporting the band through yet another critical year. He assisted the committee whilst they straightened out the discrepancies in the financial records, gave extra funding where he could, straightened out the VAT situation and also claimed for the lost bass trombone. Mr Durham organised some ties and banners for the band and make huge, personal efforts to get the band back onto the right track. Thank you, Mr Durham.

In the shadow of all of this our old friend, Ted Sutton, was ill. Perhaps it was just as well that he wasn't around the bandroom at this time. He did recover and return to the band, but not whilst this turmoil was going on, thankfully.

The band auditioned a number of conductors during the spring and summer of 1989, all to no avail. The Junior Band conductor, Mr Ted Pratt had taken the Seniors for a few rehearsals and engagements, as had Howard Bousfield. Ken Robinson was eventually appointed conductor but had to resign because of ill health. Andrew Owenson followed for a short time and then Chris Lawn. With a succession of temporary conductors the band became very unsettled. Players were coming and going at an alarming rate. It must have been difficult to find a conductor who would be willing to take on a band with the recent past history ours had. There had been nine, or maybe even ten, official bandmasters over the previous six years, and that's not counting the bandmasters who had been auditioning, or the bandsmen who had been 'helping out'. Not an ideal record with which to tempt a quality conductor. In addition, the band was hopelessly short of regular players and also a little short on commitment.

Even in the middle of chaos the band held a barbecue, bless them, one and all. Plus, a return visit to Renfrew was being organised. Alan Morrison (Principal Cornet, Grimethorpe Colliery Band) was the band's guest soloist. The bus was booked, a plaque was bought and the Lord Mayor was asked to provide us with a suitable letter to accompany it as a gift to Renfrew Burgh Band.

The visit was considered a complete success, mainly thanks to the efforts of Mr C. Cunningham. It was deemed appropriate to place a story in the Rowntree News, describing the weekend. The committee also felt that a message should be put into the Rowntree News thanking the company for its help and assistance in the past year.

A new year dawned, 1990, things could not get worse, so the only way was up (hopefully).

Well to start with there was no improvement. The temporary conductor seems to have misunderstood what was expected of the band at an engagement in the Minster, during December 1989, although it was felt that the band had played well. The band was not responding well to this conductor and the committee decided to search for a new conductor who would be able to take them to the Area Contest. Several names were mentioned and all were to be approached to ascertain their availability.

The band, meantime, was still haemorrhaging players faster than it was attracting them. Something had to be done and immediately. Advertisements were placed in the local music centre for players and the British Bandsman as well as the Yorkshire Evening Press. Once more for the second year in succession it was decided not to enter the Area Contest.

The band felt it needed to have more publicity, in order to raise interest in the band. This might lead to more players being interested in joining. So the committee agreed that a Publicity Officer was needed and Sam Kind volunteered. He ensured that the local paper ran regular articles about the band over the next few months.

This seems to have helped considerably, no doubt along with several other measures and by June 1990 the band had several new players and a new Musical Director – Mr Derek Warley. Could stability finally have come back to the band?

The company was celebrating 100 years on the Haxby Road site and decided to hold a concert in the Rowntree Theatre during September. Rowntrees commissioned a commemorative piece of music composed by Goff Richards. It was entitled 'Confection for Brass'.

This piece was performed at the Commemorative concerts held between 19th and 22nd September. Here is the front cover of the programme:

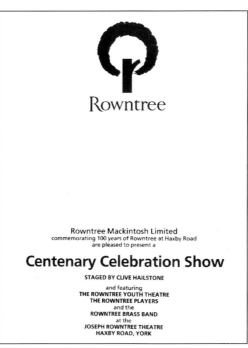

Rowntree

Rowntree Mackintosh Limited
commemorating 100 years of Rowntree at Haxby Road
are pleased to present a

Centenary Celebration Show

STAGED BY CLIVE HAILSTONE

and featuring
THE ROWNTREE YOUTH THEATRE
THE ROWNTREE PLAYERS
and the
ROWNTREE BRASS BAND
at the
JOSEPH ROWNTREE THEATRE
HAXBY ROAD, YORK

Below is the inside cover, showing the full programme which the band played and listing the band members. You should be able to find the names of three members of the current band – Sally Birch, Paul Kind and Charles Wilson. Sitting there on 3rd Cornet is Ted Sutton, still playing almost seventy years after first joining the band. Ted's only break in his membership of the band was a short period, during the Second World War, when he was on active service.

Rowntree Brass Band

THE SOUND OF BRASS
Musical Director Derek Warley

Fox from the North .... by Jacob de Haan
(based on a theme by Bert Tinge)

To a Wild Rose .... by Edward MacDowell
arr. Eric Ball
(soloist Eileen O'Hanlen)

Flashdance .... arr. Michael Briggs
(from the popular musical film **Flashdance**)

Love Changes Everything .... by Andrew Lloyd Webber
arr. Stephen Bulla
(from the hit West End musical **Aspects of Love**)

Confection of Brass .... by Goff Richards
(specially commissioned by Rowntree Mackintosh Limited for their Centenary)

The Members of the Rowntree Brass Band are
Solo Cornet Stephen Outhwaite, Charles R Wilson, Sally Birch, Tim Oldroyd,
Kevin Buridge. **Soprano Cornet** John Millson. **Repiano Cornet** Alan P Webber.
Second Cornet Michael Brown, Steve Jackson. **Third Cornet** Edward Sutton,
Liam McGough. **Solo Horn** Angela Millson. **First Horn** Frank Dawson.
Second Horn Beverley Millson. **Euphoniums** Eileen O'Hanlon, Lee G Durrant.
Baritones Paul M Gibson, Audrey Brown. **Solo Trombone** Lee Muncaster.
Second Trombone Carl Holmes, Mark S Camidge. **Bass Trombone** Robert Chilton.
Eb Basses John M Ledger, Patrick W Hunter. **Bb Basses** Trevor Collins, Paul Kind.
Percussion Norman Robinson.

ROWN
TREE

YORK

There is another name, hidden amongst this list – Audrey Brown. Audrey, as you will see if you consult the 'Behind the Stand' section, is conductor of both the Concert Band and the Beginner's Band. Mrs Brown devotes an enormous amount of time to the training of these two bands. Over the years many senior band players have developed their skills in the 'junior' band, and as an organisation we consider them our future.

That rounds up most of the calmer events of 1990. The band did several concerts during the year and took part in a contest, but the least said about that the better.

Looming hopefully on the horizon was 1991. The band had a new conductor who was pulling the band round. Maybe he had an 'artistic' temperament and a few players did object and leave, but he was talented, enthusiastic and more importantly – he was there.

The band set off immediately into two contests, firstly at Peterlee and then the North of England Area. Having been out of the competition area for the past two years the band had been demoted to the 3rd Section. One might have expected that they could hold their own at this level, but there were in fact no results worth recording, but they were at least entering again after a very bleak period. After all 'if you aren't in it, you can't win it'.

The bandroom was being overhauled – something to do with a lift shaft which was not to pass through it! This left the room with very poor ventilation and no source of natural light. Despite discussions between A. Durham and the architects at the time and two air conditioning units being put in subsequently, this room remained 'too hot' right up until we left it in April, 2003.

New players were 'signing' for the band. Old uniforms were getting the brush up and being sold off, a few new instruments had been bought and generally the band was getting tidied up again. The arrival of some new players had a strange effect on some of the established members. They felt insecure! The committee agreed in March 1991 that a set of guidelines should be drawn up to cover the introduction of a new member, it read:

a) *A player will be approached by the Committee or they will approach the band.*

b) *Before a players is asked to attend a rehearsal the player or section leader where the new one is to sit will be approached and asked for their comments.*

c) *If the existing player has no worries regarding the new player they will then be asked to come down for a rehearsal.*

d) *If the new player wishes to join the band after a rehearsal then the matter is put to the rest of the band for their comments.*

e). *If the band agrees then the new player will be asked to join the band*

These guidelines may have been agreed only twelve years ago, but it is amazing to see how out of date they seem.

The alterations to the bandroom were causing considerable frustration this year. The band had written again to the company but not much had happened to resolve the situation as it was thought to be a very political situation with no one person at the Company prepared to accept that the room was not as user friendly as it might have been. Sadly, the band was aware that they had no real power to demand action and they had no hold over the company. In the end there was nothing to do but move back in and accept the inadequacy of the facilities. A good bandroom all but ruined.

However Trevor Collins, a builder and musician in the band was currently working for someone who ran a recording studio. He had information on the costs, to the band, of making a recording. It would cost £10 per hour to hire the studio and 90p per tape. Apparently, there was no minimum number of tapes which had to be guaranteed. Sounds like a bargain to me. It was thought advisable to consult with Mr Warley (MD) to get his opinion on the matter and discuss a possible time scale and programme material. Mr Warley felt that the band was not ready, at this time, to make a recording. After the past few years, I consider he was probably correct.

The band's situation was improving gradually. Some very good local player's were being tempted to join and they really made a difference. A band doesn't need to be full of star players to enable it to improve. Finances were still very tight and there were several new instruments needed – a euphonium for the newly recruited Mike Pratt, a trombone and tenor horn. Money was so tight that instruments were being part-exchanged in order to be able to afford the new ones.

It was still felt that the profile of the band needed to be raised and so as part of the York Festival planned for 1992 the band wanted to have its own contest. The suggestion was for a solo contest in the morning, a workshop in the afternoon and an evening concert with all those involved in the earlier sessions taking part. This would, it was hoped, develop the band's image, and enable it to develop in other fields beside 'music'. I'm sure I remember a line in a famous film which says something along the lines of 'it's music that matters, only music'.

The secretary, Charles Wilson, also pointed out that in 1993 the Band was going have existed for 90 years and that perhaps a continental tour could be organised in celebration of this. This suggestion was eclipsed by the news that the conductor had been approached to take up the stick by two, higher profile, bands. He was to let the committee know when his mind was made up. In encouragement he pointed out that a year ago the band was 2nd Section, now it could go further.

A new bass trombone player, Alistair Brown, was keen to join the band and as he was considering buying his own trombone this was of double interest to the committee. The band had 'lost' a trombone, if you remember, and whilst the insurance had been sorted out, the resulting money had been used in other ways to support the needs of the band. To begin with, any way, Alistair used the old Bach Stradivarius trombone. Only a short while before, the band had been going to trade this trombone in, fortunately, the company to whom the offer was made pointed out the quality of the instrument and the band reconsidered its decision and kept it.

It shouldn't need to be pointed out that without 'jobs' for the band, there was never going to be enough money from the company to keep replacing instruments. So once again the band put its best foot forward into giving concerts and pulling money in to be able to purchase the instruments it so badly needed. All the while, the company gave a grant to the band of £1,000 per year. Although by now that barely covered the cost of employing a conductor it did mean that the band didn't need to worry about that as well. The company also supported the band, as much as it could, when it came to employing potential players, or giving a bit more money so that new uniforms could be purchased.

So as 1991 drew to a close, there was a sense of anticipation. Maybe this new year of 1992 would see the band moving onwards and upwards again. New players were steadily approaching the band for membership and once again, some of the past members were asking to return. There was still one fly in the ointment, the band secretary felt that the band had been dealt with unfairly in the YHBBA contests, recently and wanted the committee to write to ask for the band to be dropped into the 4th Section. This was not approved, and he resigned as secretary.

This year the Band took 1st Prize in the North of England Area Contest – in the 2nd Section – and success brought an invitation to the Nation Finals.

CHAPTER 16

There is no better way of getting a band back on its feet than to win an important contest. The Area Contest is the biggest in most band's calendars. The only way to gain promotion to a higher section is by consistently performing well at this contest.

In explaining the way brass band 'sections' are arranged, a basic comparison can be made with the football divisions. The premiership (football) equates neatly with the championship (brass bands) and each has a first, second, third and fourth divisions/sections (or the equivalent). Where the comparison heads in opposite directions is when comparing how promotions or demotions occur. A football team plays all season, twice a week, gaining points, winning or losing on the day, but always with the hope that the next game might be better. In the world of brass bands, the Area results over 3 consecutive years decide the fate of a band. So that's a total of, roughly, 30 – 40 minutes of performance, based on 3 years of preparation. Not quite like football anymore is it?

As you can see, therefore, gaining 1st Prize, in the 1992 Area Contest, went a long way to improve the bands' position within the 2nd Section. Having not taken part in the 1989 and 1990 contests the band was dangerously short on points to avoid demotion. Coming third in the 1991 Annual Grading Contest permitted the band to compete in the Second Section of the North of England Areas in 1992.

This year also saw the company change hands and become a division of Nestle. There were issues here which affected the band, such as VAT, and who owned the band instruments. Two diverse issues but of critical importance to the band at this time of huge financial crisis. The cost of attending the National Finals is enormous. There is the travel and accommodation for a weekend to organise, for an entire brass band (and any family members who want to come). With the change of company came a period of some 14 months where the usual 'grant' to the band had not been received and the finances were at rock bottom. The band assistant treasurer was even paying some of the band expenses out of her own money.

The instruments, who owned them? There was a question. According to Rowntree Mackintosh, the band owned the instruments. The VAT inspector advised Nestle that they were a company asset. Who was right? Well they both were in effect. The situation, once clarified seems to be that the instruments are 'owned' by the band (not the members) and so if the members decided to leave and form another band, they would not be able to use these instruments The instruments would have to remain in the bandroom until such times as another band formed there! Now that's nice and clear, isn't it?

In the midst of all this political wrangling there was great sadness.

The band lost their longest serving bandsman Ted Sutton. Ted passed away in October 1992. The band were honoured to play at his funeral.

An obituary was sent to the British Bandsman which read:

'SUTTON, Edward

'Rowntree Brass Band report with sadness the death of Ted Sutton, aged 84 years.

'Ted Joined the Rowntree Brass Band in 1918 and had been a member of the band since that time except for war service in the Royal Navy.

'Ted was an inspirational and dedicated member of the band. He was for many years Principal Cornet and one of the most respected brass band musicians in the York area. Until his final illness Ted maintained the band's extensive library in impeccable order. His dedication to Rowntree Brass Band is a fine example to us all. Ted's cheerful presence and his sound advice on technique will be sadly missed by all the band.'

The band held a memorial concert for Ted in the Joseph Rowntree Theatre on 9th July 1993 with the proceeds being sent to Ted's favourite charity the RSPCA.

The band, by coming first in the Area Contest had received an invitation to the National Finals, representing the North of England in the Second Section and the band gained a very creditable sixth place. Under the baton of Mr Derek Warley the band seemed to be entering another period of contest success.

In fact, in 1993, the band took 1st Prize again at the North of England Areas contest, gaining another invitation to the National Finals and promotion to the 1st Section having already gained 2nd Prize at the Durham League Contest. Further success was to follow this when the band took 2nd Prize at the Peterlee Contest. It had been a long time since the band had such consistent success in contests, so they were, understandably disappointed to come 18th in the National Finals.

This year saw the band also have their first trip to Denmark to take part in the Ballerup Festival. The band members were guests of the Baldur Band. Baldur is a pun on two Danish words one meaning flat and the other meaning sharp – those of you conversant in musical terminology will understand the humour in this. This was the first of three very enjoyable trips to the Ballerup Festival which we have been on in recent years.

1993 was also the year that the crew of HMS York, paraded through the City of York, the band provided the music for the march and a lovely letter, dated 24th August 1993 to the band secretary Mrs Audrey Brown read:

'what a tremendous day Sunday was! I thought the parade was a great success and the Rowntrees Band did the City of York, HMS York and themselves proud. The music which your band provided gave the march through the city that extra touch of professionalism and I know the Guard and Ship's Company thoroughly appreciated your musical accompaniment which made it so much easier to keep in step!'

'I hope that the 4.5 inch cartridge case will serve to remind the band of our appreciation for all your efforts on Sunday. Thank you and best wishes.'

The letter was signed Paul Stone, the Captain, Third Destroyer Squadron, HMS York.

All was looking hopeful for 1994, young players were feeding through from the Junior Band, taken by Ted Pratt and were contributing well to the band. Young members were on the committee and taking very active roles in supporting the committee also. An invitation for a return visit by Ballerup Band was accepted and they were to arrive 4th June 1994.

The start of 1994 was relatively peaceful, however all of that was to change rapidly. There was a complaint that the band had played with an 'unregistered player' at the North of England Area Contest. Despite a vigorous appeal by the committee, the complaint was upheld. The result was that the band was disqualified from the contest and awarded no points to be carried forward for the next three years – a really harsh result. As the points system in the Brass Band Sections is cumulative over three years, the band was demoted back to the 2nd Section the following year. This was a really harsh result.

However, the Danish Trip was considered an outstanding success and thanks were given to Charles Wilson for his organisation of it. Due to the generosity of the band members and friends the costs had been kept to a minimum and had not impacted adversely on the band's financial position.

1994 was the year in which the Beginners Band was started. Dennis Stamp, senior bandsman, had begun a band for the children of the factory workers. This had then been widened out to any children who wished to learn to play a brass instrument. This period was a difficult one within the school system. Previously many children had been taught for a minimal fee at school but now the system had changed and lessons were charged for and instruments had to be purchased by the parents. With admirable foresight, Dennis set up the Beginners Band with a few of the oldest instruments the band owned. Dennis made it clear that he wanted no payment for this and he did a fabulous job introducing young people to the world of brass bands.

You will see from the 'Behind the Stands' Section of this book that the Beginners' Band is still going strong and also has a number of adults who are learning to play a brass instrument. For some of these players it is their first experience of playing an instrument and all seem to be enthusiastic new members.

The Slow Melody competition was still taking place annually, and now we have a section for each of the three bands. It continues to be very popular and in 2003 it took up an entire evening with each of the bands performing after its soloists had finished.

The band also performed a concert at the Galtres Centre, in Easingwold. This concert has gone on to be one of the band's favourite engagements during the year and in 2004 we will be celebrating ten year's of annual concerts there. So 1994 was a very mixed year what did 1995 have to offer?

Well, 2nd Prize at the Durham League Contest was a good start. The band was putting together a business plan to try to become a more professional organisation. The aim was to plan ahead more and not be forced into crisis management so frequently. Concerts were always popular and well attended and therefore were a good source of income. Contests on the other hand, frequently brought nothing but expense and were a drain on the limited resources. The company grant did not cover the basic expenses which the band incurred, however, it did go a long way towards keeping the band solvent.

The old favourites were back, in the June 1995 Annual General Meeting – poor attendance and insufficient help in organising transport of equipment to and from engagements. It seems to be impossible to get over these issues. The huge disappointment of relegation was by now being handled with resignation. The band had been in the 1st Section before and it would be again was the attitude. How right they were.

The young players in the band were improving rapidly and making an excellent contribution to the cornet, bass and horn sections. Unfortunately, many of these young players were now reaching the age to go off to college and university and were leaving the band. In wishing them well for the future, the conductor must have been wondering how to replace them. The conductor commented that there were times the band showed a lack of professionalism, e.g. the week before the Area Contest, when rehearsals had been poorly attended. There had also been a visit by a composer, Art Barnes. The behaviour of the band at this rehearsal had caused the conductor to submit his resignation. As a result, he felt, the band had been lucky to keep certain players!

A new name was decided upon for the band. It had been felt recently that being called Rowntree Mackintosh Brass Band had unfairly inferred to prospective sponsors that we were already well subsidised. The new name was to be *City of York Rowntree Band*. I would suggest that the company must have vetoed this as I can find no record of it ever being used to publicise the band either for concerts or contests.

Baring in mind the conductor's resignation, there was some discussion at this AGM that the band was officially without a conductor. The chairman, Trevor Collins, asked the conductor, Derek Warley, if he had had further thoughts regarding his decision and after further discussion Mr Warley decided to reverse his decision and was again appointed the band's Director of Music.

The second band trip to Denmark was being arranged for August 1995 and the band needed to get themselves organised. There were E11 forms, passports and travel to arrange. The representative from Baldur

Band visited during early July to finalise the programme details as at least one joint concert was going to take place. Once the programmes list and concert details were finalised the conductor would decide on the music for each concert. Mr Durham, Nestle, had also offered to arrange a concert through the Danish Nestle Branch.

Several social events were also being planned for during 1995, a treasure hunt; a golf tournament (which has become an annual event); a quiz; a barbecue and a party at 'Melodies'.

The trip to Denmark during August however was the highlight of the band year. It did much to raise the morale of the band who were so disappointed at being demoted, in their minds, very unfairly. Here is a photograph, courtesy of Frank Dawson, of one of the open air concerts the band gave:

Principal Cornet in the photograph is Sally Birch, who was the Principal, prior to joining the army. On her return from Army training Sally became Principal again. Sally then left the Band to do her State Registered Nurse training. Since returning to the band in 2002 Sally has been happy to play a variety of parts in the cornet section, as needed.

So, we can close the door on a very tough time for the band, for now. It will be nice to be able to concentrate on a run of nice things for a change and as our progress to the Championship Section begins with 4th place at the 1996 North of England Areas Contests (2nd Section) this is a good place to start.

CHAPTER

17

Fourth place, North of England Areas, 1996 (2nd Section). Preceded by a 3rd Prize at the Durham League Contest and followed by a 3rd Prize at the Peterlee Contest, now we are back on track.

The Danish band, Baldur Band was coming over in the summer for a second return visit. At the end of the summer though, the band was facing another exodus of young players to universities and colleges. New players were needed and had to be found, either from the Training Band or from elsewhere.

The situation regarding further sponsorship, perhaps from the City Council had gone nowhere other than the Leisure Services agreeing we would be an asset to York.

At the AGM in April 1996, the chairman raised the point that the business plan the band had been working on for some time had been sent off to the City of York Council. Although no response had been received it was thought important that the band took on board all the details of the plan and everyone should become involved in bringing it to fruition.

The Learners' Group, started by Dennis Stamp, was mentioned as being very successful and we needed more instruments for this group. The chairman said that work must now proceed in sending off Grant Applications and he thanked Dennis for all his efforts with the Learners Group and also thanked Ted Pratt for all his work with the Training Band (which recently had regularly been producing players for the senior band). The Beginners' Band received a grant of £350, thanks to Dennis and was able to purchase some suitable music and a second hand instrument or two.

At the same meeting the conductor said that the playing in Denmark was first class and so had been the concerts with again this year a complete change of programme. He said the band was not aware of the amount of work that needed to go in to finding new and different music. He sent his thanks to Ray (Rochester, Librarian) for his work and help. He further agreed that the youth policy of the band was showing results and congratulations and thanks were passed to Ted and Dennis for their support in this. Soon there was to be a concert to show off all three of the bands.

During the summer of 1996 the band played at a special wedding ceremony. The wedding was of one of our percussionists, Rachel Berry and Charles Wilson, sometimes cornet/baritone/horn player. At about this same time the conductor was causing some concern to the committee. It seems he was taking another band and there was some conflict with rehearsals and contest arrangements. The replacement conductor, nominated by Derek, was not always turning up and the situation needed to be resolved. The matter was to be discussed with the band.

This was the year that I joined the band in September, so I hope to be able to put a more personal spin on these last few years in the first hundred years of the band's history.

The contest results in 1997 were also encouraging. A 2nd Prize at the Durham League and a 4th Place in the North of England Area Contest, following by a 4th Place in the St Helen's Contest. The year was rounded off nicely with a 4th Place at the Malton Entertainment Contest.

1998 saw an improvement in the North of England Area Contest. The band came 1st gaining an invitation to the National Finals and also promotion to the 1st Section. It had only taken four years but finally the band was back in this section again. Whilst the National Finals, in Nottingham saw us gain only 14th place the band thoroughly enjoyed the experience and on return took 4th Prize at the Easingwold Marching Contest.

The band has habitually over recent times taken part in the Whit Friday Marching Contests and below is a photograph, courtesy of Frank Dawson of the band at one of the contests:

Nearest to the camera, from right to left is Charles Wilson, Frank Dawson and me (Sharon Lang).

We had a change of conductor during this year. Mr Warley decided to move on to pastures new and Mr Chris Hirst auditioned for the post at the recommendation of Ted Pratt and was duly appointed. With Chris we recorded our first (and so far only) CD entitled 'Confection for Brass'. Readers may remember that this piece had been written to celebrate the company's 100 years in York at the Haxby Road site. The recording was dedicated 'to Ted'. Mr Ted Pratt one time solo cornet player, Junior Band Conductor, Senior Band Conductor and overall Band stalwart who died a few months before the record was made. He was a fine bandsman. His son, Mike Pratt is still Principal Euphonium with the band and Grace, his widow, who appeared earlier in this book, still supports the Band at concerts and contests. With her experience of brass bands her views are held in high regard.

During 1999 the band continued with this our contest success in the North of England Area Contest (1st Section) not only did we win 2nd Prize and an invitation to the National Finals but we also won the Best Basses Prize. We came 7th in the Finals in Harrogate and also came 2nd in the Malton Entertainment Contest later in the year.

The band purchased a 'walking out' uniform this year, so that when we are travelling as a band to and from engagements or contests we look smart and professional. We had a plain navy coloured jacket and teamed this with the Nestle tie. Following one of our many concerts in Copmanthorpe the band, en masse, went into the local public house. Several of the regulars asked if we were the crew from an airline,. Being 25 miles from the nearest airport that seems a bit unlikely to me.

We had a great time during the middle part of the year when we had the opportunity to work with Mr Michael Aspel and surprise an ex-Rowntree employee in a special edition of 'This is Your Life'.

Fred Stewart, MBE, was the recipient of the surprise and the band was honoured to be asked to march through Heslington to surprise him and then spend the rest of the day as guests of the studio before playing again at the end of the programme.

Here is the band, on the set of the TV programme playing, 'Congratulations':

The bass player at the far right (rear) of the band is actually the conductor, Mr Chris Hirst (trombonist!). The Principal Cornet player here is Mark Durham, who was our principal until he headed for university in September 2002.

Towards the end of August 1999, the band made a third visit to the Ballerup Festival as guests of the Baldur Band. The Baldur Band were excellent hosts and had organised a number of outings and concerts on behalf of Nestle Rowntree Band. Once there we were able to relax and enjoy the experience thanks to the wonderful organisation and planning that had taken place between Baldur band and Mr and Mrs Ken Stamp. Here is a photograph of this, most recent visit, showing a joint band concert during the Festival itself:

Our band is on the left of the photograph and the Baldur Band is on the right. The conductor for this tour was Mr Graham Walker, who did an excellent job and found a superb balance between allowing the band to enjoy the experience but still taking the rehearsals and concerts seriously.

In 2000 we came 4th in the North of England Areas (1st Section). This same year saw the band participate in the 'York Millennium Symphony of Brass and Bells' with music written by L. Barber. This was a tremendously ambitious project involving all the brass bands in York and the bells of no less than 12 churches in York, including the Minster. Various groups from the brass bands were perched high on buildings looking over the city. Members of the public were invited to walk around the city during the evening performance to appreciate the sounds made over the 90 minutes. It was a most unusual and interesting performance for all concerned.

We came 4th again the following year and gained promotion to the Championship Section for the first time in the band's long and varied history. Then we had another change of conductor in 2001. Mr Hirst departed for pastures greener and eventually, after a very trying time, we appointed Mr William Rushworth as our Musical Director.

The band took a risk with Billy. We were to be the first band that he was responsible for as a conductor, but it is a risk that has paid off. 2001 also saw the band perform extremely well at the Brighouse March and Hymn Contest, where the band competed against some of the very best brass bands in the country and ultimately came 10th out of 23. This was a terrific result for a newly promoted band.

The band had been relatively stable for the past few years without too much coming and going, rehearsals had been well attended and progress had been consistent and rewarding as a result. The largest set back we had was in 2002 when our entire set of banners was stolen along with one of the band's tenor horns (and the music pad). This resulted in the band having to perform without banners for the next fourteen months until all the insurance details were sorted out and our concert in Copmanthorpe, during April 2003 was the first outing for our brand new banners.

Competing in the Championship Section for the first time ever, was always going to be difficult for us and we gained 8th place (out of 8 competing bands) in the 2002 North of England Area Contest.

Not happy with that we went on to take 3rd Prize at the Malton Entertainment Contest. The year was capped out in fine style with a fantastic result at the Hardraw Scar Contest where the band swept the board and received 1st Prize (March Contest); 1st Prize (Hymn Contest); 1st Prize (Selection) and obviously Mr Rushworth won the Best Conductor's Prize.

We have improved our position in the Championship Section this year, 2003, by coming 5th out of the 10 bands which took part. You cannot imagine the effect this had on the band. Had you been there you would have been forgiven for thinking that we had won the contest. In a way we had. As ever, if we had performed less well, on that day, we would have been demoted, back down to the 1st Section, and there wasn't a man or woman on the stage who was prepared to go down without a fight.

So, that completes our first hundred years. A truly remarkable story of highs and lows. However, through all the century that the band has existed we have been fortunate in having the same sponsor. Without this support the band would have floundered right from the start. We believe we may be the only band to still have its original sponsors.

Anyway here's to the next 100 years and as I said in the beginning, make no mistake . We've only just begun.

SECTION **2**

Behind the Stand

Senior Band

William Rushworth – Conductor, 2001 to present day

I was born in Dewsbury (Yorkshire), but spent my early childhood in Australia where I began playing the guitar aged 9.

I can, justifiably claim to come from a legendary brass band family and had decided against learning a brass instrument, thinking that my family history would be too hard an act to follow…

My Great Uncle William was a cornet player with Black Dyke before moving to Principal cornet with Besses of the Barn, and then he became Principal Trumpet with the orchestra of the Covent Garden, until his death in 1958.

My Great Uncle Donald was a professional violinist and also played Bass with Brighouse & Rastrick.

My paternal Grandfather was second to none as a tenor horn player initially with Black Dyke and then (as solo horn) with Carlton Main, Brighouse, St Hilda's Professional Band and finally with Bickershaw Colliery.

My Uncle Charlie was the Champion Cornet Player of Great Britain, in 1947.

My father, Ken, was also a fine trombonist, latterly of Markham Main Colliery.

My maternal Grandfather, George, was also a good trombonist.

An even earlier ancestor (also William) was the resident conductor of Black Dyke in the 1860's, along with 7 more of the family as playing members.

Eventually I began to play a brass instrument, the cornet, with the City of Enfield and Kensington and Norwood Bands.

I was an enthusiastic fan when the James Shepherd Versatile Brass toured Australia, in 1978. So much so that, when we returned to England I became Principal Cornet of Queensbury Music Centre Band (which was founded by James Shepherd).

My next move saw me appointed Principal Cornet with the Markham Main Colliery Band followed by a move to Carlton Main Frickley Colliery Band, on Repiano. It was whilst at Frickley that I moved onto tenor horn and became the band's Solo Horn player. This was a huge move, in more ways than one, I had the burden of my Grandfather's huge reputation to live up to. (Editors note – William managed not only to live up to his Grandfather's reputation but has become the finest horn player of his generation.)

When I moved to Hammonds (as Solo Horn), under Geoffrey Whitham, my career began to blossom. I have played Solo Horn with Black Dyke Mills Band – winning the British Open in 1992, YBS Leyland, Cory and Stocksbridge. I have twice been declared winner of the prestigious soloist award at the 'Brass in Concert' Championships (Spennymoor) and in 1999 recorded my first solo CD – 'The Classic Horn Collection' – with the JJB Sports Leyland Band. On 3 successive occasions I have held the title 'Horn Champion of Great Britain (having only competed 3 times) as well as being the horn player of the British Open Champions (again on 3 successive occasions. I am very proud, also, to have been Principal Horn with the Battle Creek Brass Band (USA) for 8 years.

Since taking up the stick in front of Nestlé Rowntree Band we have gained promotion to the Championship Section, for the first time in the band's long history and took every prize at the 2002 Hardraw Scar Contest.

Currently, I am also the Musical Director of Carlton Main Frickley Colliery Band and we recently took 1st Prize in the Southern Counties Open Contest and won the award for the winning conductor.

During the day – I am a self-employed building contractor.

Sally Birch (2nd Solo Cornet 2), joined 1984

I was born in York in 1975 and attended Westfield Junior School where I was given the opportunity to start playing cornet at the age of 8 (a decision keenly supported by my music loving family). I progressed through the Royal School of Music's grade system and was then persuaded to join Rowntree junior band at the age of 9, by my brass teacher – Ted Pratt. I was also a member of 2 York Youth bands and attended many tours around Europe (a real start to my passion for music and travelling!).

Staying with Rowntree Band, I joined the senior band and became Principal cornet at the age of 16 (a position I kept for 5 successful years and helped win many Second section contests).

Within this time, I also joined the army (at the age of 18) as a professional musician in the Adjutant General's Corp. Leaving the army, I decided to undertake nurse training in Nottingham for 3 years, when I didn't play an instrument at all.

I came back to York as a qualified nurse in 2000, aged 24, and on hearing the Championship section Nestlé Rowntree Band in concert, I just could not resist rejoining!

I am now 27 and have been playing again in the band for nearly 2 years (as 3rd cornet, Flugel horn and now Solo Cornet 2). I met my current partner, Gordon Hill, in the band and just love being able to play music to such a high standard in this excellent band.

I have played a brass instrument for the past 18 years and hope to continue for the rest of my life.

Leo Castro (Bass Trombone), joined 1998

I started to learn to play the trombone in October, 1997 and joined the Concert Band in February, 1998 on 2nd Trombone.

I enjoyed a spell playing Solo Trombone, with the Concert Band,. I was invited to play with the Senior Band in 1999 and joined properly in 2000 on 2nd Trombone (Senior Band). At the beginning of 2003 I was moved to Bass Trombone and am really looking forward to playing the parts.

I have private lessons on the trombone and passed my ASBRM Grade 5 last year. I also play the piano and am working towards Grade 5 on it in the future. I used to play the flute and had lessons at school, for a while I played in my school band.

Currently, I am in Year 11 at school and preparing for my GCSE's, this summer, I hope to do A-levels and eventually study at university.

I enjoy playing the trombone with Nestlé Rowntree Band and hope to continue playing when I leave York and throughout the rest of my life, as I have got to know some good people through music.

Andrew Clark (Repiano Cornet)joined 1992

I first learned to play the cornet when a band was set up in my primary school (Headlands P.S., Haxby), when I was about 8 years old. After a year or so I joined the Rowntree Junior Band.

In 1992, my peripatetic teacher, (and the then conductor of the junior band) Ted Pratt, recommended that I be moved up to the senior band, where I started on 3rd cornet.

My first contest, in 1993, was the areas in which we progressed to the national Finals in London. From then on I became an ever present member of the band, progressing from 3rd cornet to 2nd, Repiano, and finally (by 1997) Soprano cornet.

In 1998 I left the band to go to Sheffield Hallam University, to study History. Despite being away at university, I still managed to play soprano at the National Finals in 1998, Flugel horn at the areas in 1999 and cornet again in the National Finals in 1999.

On finishing university, I came back to York and rejoined the band – playing Repiano cornet again.

Bruce Davies (3rd Cornet) joined 2001

I started to learn the cornet in 1994 at North Duffield Primary School. I soon joined my first band at Selby Music Centre and played there for 7 years. Last year, when I left, I was the principal cornet player.

I joined Selby Wind Band when I started Selby High School and for a while played Eb bass, but I had to give it up when I joined Nestlé Rowntree Band.

I had only been playing with Nestlé Rowntree Band for 2 or 3 weeks when I took part in my first contest, Malton Entertainment Contest, I was 'dropped in the deep end' by having to play the 3rd cornet part on my own! As the annual areas contest approached I had just about got to grips with brass band playing and enjoyed being able to play the part relatively well... eventually, when we attended the Whit Friday Marches. That was when I discovered how embarrassingly bad I am at marching!!!

In the summer of 2002, Mark and Andrew Durham and I (whom I knew from Nestlé Rowntree Band and also the Barlby Foot Tappers band) embarked on the 'Coast to Coast' walk. Our aim was to raise money for a girl with Spinal Muscular Atrophy. The walk began from St. Bees in Cumbria and ended at Robin Hood's Bay in North Yorkshire – a total distance of 192 miles – it took us 10 days. We all enjoyed it tremendously, although we struggled hugely, and raised over £600.

At the moment I am studying A-Levels at Selby College in Maths, Physics and Chemistry. This summer, unfortunately, I will be leaving the band as I am going to university to study Physics. However, I hope to keep in touch and might hopefully make a reappearance!

Kevin Dickson-Lane (Principal Cornet) joined 1999

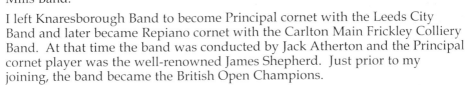

I started to play a brass instrument at the age of 7, becoming principal cornet with the Knaresborough Silver Band at the age of 12.

I was taught to play the cornet by my father who was a trombone player with the band, he also taught my elder brother Patrick to play the cornet. Patrick went on to become the Principal cornet player with The Band of The Coldstream Guards, Yorkshire Imperial Band and Assistant Principal with Black Dyke Mills Band.

I left Knaresborough Band to become Principal cornet with the Leeds City Band and later became Repiano cornet with the Carlton Main Frickley Colliery Band. At that time the band was conducted by Jack Atherton and the Principal cornet player was the well-renowned James Shepherd. Just prior to my joining, the band became the British Open Champions.

In my early twenties I joined the West Riding County Fire Service. In 1995 I took early retirement, as Assistant Chief Fire Officer with the Devon Fire and Rescue Service. During that time I ceased playing the cornet and decided to take it up again shortly before my retirement.

I moved back to Yorkshire with my family in 1997 and joined the British Steel Teesside Band as Assistant Principal Cornet. Then I held a similar position with East Yorkshire Motor Services Band (EYMS) before joining the Nestlé Rowntree Band in 1999.

I was educated at the Harrogate Technical College and was trained as an Electrical Engineer before joining the Fire Service. I am currently employed, on a part-time basis (3 days per week), by June Emerson (Wind Music) – who are publishers with a worldwide client base.

I thoroughly enjoy playing for Nestlé Rowntree Band and hope to continue for many years to come, although probably not as Principal cornet.

Andrew Durham (Percussion) joined 1997

I first became interested in playing percussion aged 8 (1991).

My chance to become the next Phil Collins didn't come until the following year when I was asked if I wanted to start playing for the school band. At that time it was the Barlby Primary School Band but it is now known as the Barlby Foottappers Band. Since joining the band, 12 years ago, I have been to four different countries (France, Germany, Greece and Ireland), playing in some world famous places such as Disneyland, Paris.

Over the last 12 enjoyable years I have also played with the Selby Music Centre, Pit bands for school productions and recently a group of about 10 started a dance band. I started playing with Rowntree Junior Band in 1996 and advanced to the Senior band a year later.

During this hectic period I still had school and then college work to do. I left school with 9 GCSE's. When at school I found the perfect job, as a game keeper, through my work experience. I went to Bishop Burton College to study Countryside Management. In the college holidays I kept returning to Escrick Park Estate to help the head game keeper.

When I went to college I had to move away from home, unfortunately, and I had to leave the band. I kept in touch with the band and helped them out at competitions and concerts when they needed me. I finished college 2 years ago (2001) with a National Diploma in Countryside Management.

After leaving college I went back to Escrick Park as the under-keeper and returned to Nestlé Rowntree Band. The following year I got laid off from Escrick Park (through no fault of mine) so this meant I had to find another job, and I did. It was on a game farm at Pately Bridge. This meant I had early mornings and late nights to do and I was unable to finish work and get to band on time. So once again I had to leave the band, but still continued to help out from time to time.

It is now 2003 and I have re-joined the Nestlé Rowntree Band and I'm still enjoying playing percussion 12 years down the line.

Mark Durham (Principle /Soprano) 1993 - present

I started playing at Barlby County Primary School, aged 8, under Ted Pratt, Father of Mike. I was one of the first five members of the Barlby Foottappers Band and have played with them ever since, touring France and Dublin.

The first Brass Band I played with was the York Railway Institute Golden Rail Band. I started playing second cornet and over the next eighteen months I progressed to the position of principal cornet. I remained with the band until I was 13 at which point I moved to my current band, Rowntrees. I have played second cornet, third man down on solo cornet, and under the bands direction of Chris Hirst, I was promoted to

the position of principle cornet, having taken over from Fraser Hill in 1997.
I was principle for 4 years, and I am currently playing soprano for the band.
How long this will last I do not know, it may be over sooner than I think.

I have played for the North Yorkshire Schools County Youth Band in the years
1993, 1994 under Graham Walker and Frank Renton, touring Scotland and the
North of England. I played with Selby Music Centre for 9 years where I
worked my way up to top man of the senior band. I have played in pit
orchestra's and have helped out many other bands and made some great
friends (and some not so good).

In 1999 I had an audition with the world famous Brighouse and Rastrik Band,
and played with them at several concerts. This certainly being one of my
favourite moments as it was one of my early ambitions as a youngster.

I am currently studying at Newcastle University and sadly I am not able to
attend as much as I would like, but unfortunately for the band I WILL BE
BACK. The only ambition I have left in playing really is to play in the Albert
Hall with the Rowntree Band, who knows this might be our year, fingers
crossed.

Sharon Fallon (Flugel Horn) joined 1996

I was born in York and so far I have always been a resident.
I currently live in Strensall with my husband, Nick, and son,
James. Before I got married, my surname was Greenfield.
I work for the City of York Council as a Clerical Assistant
within Parking Services.

My brass band career started when I was 4. My brother,
Stephen, was at the time learning to play Tenor Horn at the Railway Institute
Beginners' Band, until our parents bought him his own cornet. I used to try to
blow a note though it every now and then. Stephen eventually taught me to
play the 'C' scale and at the age of 5 I began playing cornet with the Beginners'
Band.

My parents were introduced to Ted Pratt, who at the time was conductor of
the 'Railway's' senior band. He taught Stephen and me every Sunday
morning until I reached the age of 17. Ted also taught at the York Music
Centre on Saturday mornings, so when I was able, I joined the Concert Band
and the Dance Band.

After 3 years of playing I moved in the 'Railway's' Training Band and
progressed through the ranks of the cornet section until I became Principal at
13 years of age. Apart from playing solos, I was also given the task of playing
'The Last Post' and 'Revallie' at every Remembrance service – I recall we did 3
services each year: at Easingwold; Duncombe Place Cenotaph and Market
Weighton.

I also played with the Yorkshire and Humberside Youth Band – because it
would only meet and rehearse once a month, I was able to continue with all 3
bands until leaving school.

At 16 I was asked to join the Railway Institute Intercity Band (Senior Band), who at the time competed in the North East Area Championship Section. I was given a position on Solo Cornet and after 6 months became principal. Three years later I left to take a complete break from playing.

Sometime later, by chance, I met up with a band colleague who used to play with the Railways Institute, he was by then playing with Rowntree. I was told they were short of a 2nd cornet for a contest which was being held 3 weeks later. I offered to stand in for them and ended up staying. I was moved to Solo Cornet a month later and played there for a couple of years until I was asked to give the Tenor Horn a go, due to shortage of players. I stayed on 1st horn for about a year but preferred cornet and moved back.

Roughly 2 years ago the band's Flugel horn player left, so the position needed to be filled. I jokingly offered to try and 2 days later I was given the instrument. It has been one of the best decisions I have made so far, I absolutely love the flugel.

Early last year I married my partner, Nick, and was very touched that the band could play at our wedding. Most of the guests have told me since that they thought the band was wonderful. Later in the year I took a 6 month break from playing as I was expecting our son, James, who was born in July. When James was about 5 weeks old I returned to the cornet section, but was asked a few weeks later to go back onto Flugel, which I was delighted to do, and am continuing to do.

I have to say that, since having my son, without the understanding and support of my husband and family, it would be very hard for me to continue doing what I love, playing in the Nestlé Rowntree Band.

Aidan (Aidie) Foster (2nd Baritone) joined 2001

Well here are a few words about me and how I became interested in brass banding.

I started playing the Euphonium at the age of 9, at school. I was lucky enough to have peripatetic music lessons, at school, from Jim Shepherd. I quickly progressed through the basics of playing and it wasn't long before I joined my first Brass band, Jayess 87.

After playing Solo Euphonium with them for only a short time I moved up to Jayess Junior band where I stayed for 3-4 years. After gaining the Solo Euphonium position I was asked to join the Jayess Queensbury Band, who were currently playing in the Championship Section. It was here that I first experienced a Championship Test piece – 'Partita'.

At the age of 18 I left Jayess Queensbury, and playing, as I went away to university. This break in my playing didn't last long. I was asked by one of my friends to join their band, Barnsley Building Society, to help out for the Areas and Coal Board Championships.

I seemed to keep coming in and out of 'retirement' to play at various contests even playing Bb Bass one year! I then left Barnsley as I was too busy at university and was planning a trip abroad once I graduated.

On returning from my travels it wasn't long before I was hunted down and asked to play again, this time for Tingley. Despite not playing full time for some 4 years I soon was given the responsibility of Solo Euphonium. Unfortunately my time at Tingley was only short as I started a new job with shift work which made it impossible to keep playing.

After another break from playing of 4 years I was approached, by the same friend as before, and asked to help out at Nestlé Rowntree Band for the Areas. That was 1 year ago and I'm still coming to as many rehearsals as possible and helping out at all contests.

Adrian Gibbs (Eb Bass) joined 2002

I was born in South Wales, but was brought up in Harrogate.

I started playing the bass back in 1982, which I was told there was a spare bass with Tewit Youth Band. I was a member there until I turned 19 (the maximum age), then I had to retire. Unfortunately, I didn't look to join another band.

Following a chance meeting, in 2002, with an old friend from Tewit, I came to a rehearsal with Nestlé Rowntree Band and have loved it here ever since.

I am currently working as a kitchen, bedroom and bathroom consultant for Magnet. Between work and rehearsals, my wife and I are expecting our first child in May. We are also both busy updating the old farmhouse we live in, in Arkendale.

Fraser Hill (Solo Cornet 3) joined 1994

I started playing the cornet in 1974 at Primary School in Paisley, Scotland, and joined the Barrhead Burgh Band on 3rd cornet, though for the first few weeks I didn't have an instrument and had to just sit and watch the others! I played with the Barrhead Band for 8 years eventually moving onto Soprano Cornet in the late seventies.

In 1981 I moved to the Kirkintilloch Band and played in the Championship section for the first time. Moving back onto Bb cornet, I played with them for the next 5 years winning the Scottish Championship twice and the Scottish Quartet Title. During 1984-86 we played at the National Finals, the European Championships and competed in the BBC Best of Brass televised band contest. While with Kirkintilloch I also met my future wife, Sally, who was playing percussion whilst completing her university studies in Glasgow.

In 1986 I moved to Nottinghamshire and joined the Thoresby Colliery Band on 'bumper up'. From Thoresby I then followed my principal cornet and moved with him to the William Davis Construction Group Band where, in 1988, we won the Midland Regional Contest to qualify again for the National Finals in the Albert Hall.

In 1989 I moved to Yorkshire, rejoined Sally at the Hammonds Sauce Works band and later that year we were married . After the demise of Hammonds a few years later, I gave up playing for about a year, however in 1994 I joined the Nestlé Rowntree Band to 'help out' as a short term favour to the Musical Director at the time, Mr Derek Warley. I'm still here for the centenary celebrations and for the last few years I have been the Chairman and Contest secretary of the band.

Gordon Hill (Solo Baritone) joined 1998

I was born in Girvan on the west coast of Scotland, in 1953, and began playing a brass instrument at the age of 7 (in the Salvation Army). I was educated at Kings Park Senior Secondary School.

I played euphonium with the Parkhead Citadel (Glasgow) band until the age of 21 when I joined Newmains Colliery Band. I played with Newmains from 1975 until 1978 (the year they qualified for the Championship Finals – at the Royal Albert Hall).

In 1979 I joined Whitburn Burgh Band and we won the Scottish Championship during 1980. Later that year we played at the Royal Albert Hall – 3 times in one weekend – this has been the highlight of my playing career. Whitburn took part in the National Championships on the Saturday and then played twice on the Sunday as participants in the European Championships.

I got married in 1979, and left Scotland in 1981, to work at John Smiths Brewery. I gave up playing for 10 years (until 1991) to help bring up my family.

In 1991 I joined South Milford Band and stayed there for 4 years, before retiring again. However, in 1998, I heard Rowntree Band play at a local concert and could not resist the sound of brass. I subsequently joined the band, playing baritone, and have enjoyed the friendliness and support of the band for 5 years now and I hope to continue making music with them in the future.

Chris(tian) Horton (Eb Bass) joined 2002

Having started on the recorder at junior school like everyone else, my first blow on a brass instrument was on trombone when I was about 11. This only lasted for a couple of weeks because my school mates warned me that I would end up with 'rubber lips'. So I gave it up and carried on to learn the organ instead, having lessons with Ralph Barley in Chesterfield.

It wasn't until I was 16 that I was finally coaxed into brass banding by a girlfriend who knew I could read music. I was handed a baritone and persuaded to join the William Rhodes School Band in Chesterfield. The school band was started by David Windle who also formed the Championship senior band Rhodian Brass.

I didn't stay at William Rhodes for long because I moved to York in October 1992 to study at the university. I met Audrey Brown who worked in the university library and she offered to give me a lift down to Rowntrees. I went to a few practices but didn't join as there were too many other distractions at the university!

After uni in 1996, I moved to Tadcaster into my current job at Samuel Smith's brewery. I found the nearest band which was Wetherby and joined them on baritone. I moved onto solo Euph and in 2000 we won the 4th Section Area Contest at St George's Hall. There could not have been a better year to qualify because all the National Finals were being held at the Royal Albert Hall for the Millennium. We came about half way down the results at the finals but that didn't matter - it was a great experience for the band.

After 5 years at Wetherby I was ready for a change so in the summer of 2002 I came down to Rowntrees for another blow and this time I finally joined on Eb Bass – only 10 years after my first visit!

Ann Jackson (Solo Horn) joined 2002

I was born in Saddleworth and have 2 brothers and a sister. I am the only member of my family who plays a brass instrument.

When I was 10 years old my friend Janet (12) asked me to go along to band practise with her to Dobcross Band. Mr George Gibson was the conductor. Much to my mum's dismay I brought home a tenor horn. After about 6 months (and a lot of practise at home, with the band and Oldham Music Centre) I was playing Solo horn.

I played at Dobcross for approximately 10 years then went to Chadderton Band for a further 8 years (approx.); then to Whitworth Vale and Healy, and also played in a group called Phoenix Brass. I played at Whitworth for 10 years and with Phoenix Brass for about 6 years. During my time with Phoenix Brass we went on a 10 day tour, in 1989, it was a wonderful experience.

In 1994 I joined Marsden Silver Prize Band where I met up with Shaun Jackson, who used to play at Dobcross Band, and also went to the same school as me. In 1995 we started going out together (on Whit Friday night) by the October of that year we had bought a house in Marsden and moved in together.

I have 2 children – Lisa (21) and Daniel (18) and we are now proud grandparents to Jordan Ann (17 months).

In January, 2002, William Rushworth asked me to join Nestlé Rowntree Brand, on solo horn, and this has been the best 12 months of playing for me for a long time. They are all lovely people who enjoy playing together. We are in the Championship section and working to stay there during 2003.

I have enjoyed my 37 years banding and have met some nice people. I feel very privileged to be playing under William, at my age, and hope I can go on for a few more years.

Shaun Antony Jackson (2nd Cornet) joined 2002

I was born in Saddleworth in 1957 – I have 2 brothers and a sister.

I started to learn playing cornet while at Saddleworth school, my teacher was Brian Broadlent, who played for the Black Dyke Mills Band.

In 1970, I joined Dobcross Brass Band, under the baton of George Gibson – after two years I was offered a position in the senior band, starting at the bottom on 3rd cornet. I moved up the ranks to play repiano, but in 1974 I started work and college was on practise nights, so I left the band.

After an absence of 15 years, my youngest brother and his wife took over the stewardship of the Marsden Band room. When members of Marsden Band found out I used to play the cornet they talked me into playing again. The year was 1990, and the band was down to around fourteen players.

In 1994 Ann Lamb joined the band (she used to play in Dobcross Band all those years ago) and in 1995 we started to go out together. In October, 1995, we bought a house together in Marsden and have lived there ever since.

In 2001 I decided to retire (again) from playing – Ann carried on, but in 2002 she left Marsden Band and joined Rowntree Band. After not playing for around 8 months, I also joined Rowntree Band. I think at the moment Ann and I travel the furthest to band – around 120 miles round trip.

Paul Kind (BBb Bass) joined 1983

I started playing in Brass Bands purely by chance. So, after nearly 25 years nothing much has changed then.

My main musical interest is in jazz piano but I thought it would be easier to improvise on a trumpet rather than a keyboard. Three valves looked a whole lot simpler than 10 fingers on an 88-note piano. I mentioned this to an old friend, Charles Monk who had been a euphonium player with local silver bands in the Leicester area where I grew up. Charles had fought on the Western Front during the Great War, so he must have been in his 70s when this conversation took place. He told me that the only way to learn (and to get an instrument at the same time) was to join a brass band. Furthermore, he said that if I did join a band then he'd come along too, since he had never really lost the "bug". He got his dentures fixed, found an old mouthpiece and that was it. We were both on our way.

The Leicester Imperial Brass Band was a struggling 3rd Section band conducted by Ivor ***. His son played with William Davis Construction – so Ivor probably knew his stuff. The band was fairly desperate for players so they welcomed both of us with open arms. Charles (a recycled oldie aged about 75) and me (a complete novice aged about 25). Ivor gave me a cornet and sat me on the back row next to the Bb bass. He told me to blow when I could make a sound. A week later I had experimented sufficiently to know the principal valve combinations and that was it ! Life as a back-row cornet player stretched ahead of me. Park jobs and school fetes. Christmas carols and charity fundraisers. Then fate lent a hand.

I moved to London in 1978 and quickly learned that there were precisely TWO bands in Inner London – one at Fulham and the other at South Norwood. This latter turned out to be the Crystal Palace Brass Band and they rehearsed in a church school in Balham. The band's conductor (Mal) was a Sergeant Major with the Coldstream Guards Band. The Band's then Director, Peter Parkes, apparently approved of his musicians "moonlighting" with a Brass Band and Crystal Palace included several military bandsmen, including Ian Walsh on solo cornet. I joined as a 2nd cornet player. Rehearsals on a Wednesday night were simply terrifying. Mal made sure everyone watched him from the first downbeat to the last. Hymns from the Salvation Army book could be played at any tempo or dynamic, with changes to either thrown in at any moment. If you took your eyes off him you'd miss his cue and get a roasting for your troubles. Concentration was the name of the game – although that did not stop the solo trombone from playing 633 Squadron instead of Hawaiian Samba at one gig. As with many bands, changes in personnel created crises of all sorts. A hole in the horn section needed filling and I was "promoted" to 2nd horn. A bit scary to sit in the front row I thought – nowhere to hide. After a while I took over as Secretary to the Band, mainly running the booking side. Looking for new gigs was both exciting and challenging. The Band got all sorts of work – particularly since there was effectively no local opposition. We played television and radio. Battersea Arts Centre and the Royal Festival Hall (well outside it actually). And lots of concerts in GLC parks.

Everyone loved brass band music – or so I thought. Little clues gave the game away though. Like the night a sniper opened fire on us during rehearsal. Or the park job where the local lads built a bonfire under the bandstand. Little clues like that. I was especially pleased to get BBC Radio London to set up a Christmas Eve "Dial-a-Carol" show hosted by Robbie Vincent. We played live in the studio and Londoners phoned in with their requests. The BBC thought we were so good they booked us immediately for the following year. They also provided hospitality that flowed very freely. So freely that any notion of last-minute Christmas shopping went out the window. The "Dial-a-Carol" became a regular fixture. So much so that on the night before Christmas Crystal Palace families got used to seeing their bands folk slightly drunk and always very late in the day.

After Mal left the band and after another Neller Hall replacement, Crystal Palace encountered James Watson. By then I was playing Eb bass. The first rehearsal he took with us involved his teaching the band to breathe. Simple idea that. Upbeat equals intake. That night he introduced us to Variations on a Ninth. It was beyond us as a band then, but it became a regular rehearsal piece and we spent the last half hour of every rehearsal working on it. James was playing the odd gig with Philip Jones Brass Ensemble – including a memorable performance at the Albert Hall of Pictures at an Exhibition. He was a phenomenal band trainer, travelling down to South London from Watford. One night he brought a top soloist with him but there was only half a band present at rehearsal. And that was it ! He wished the band well and walked away.

I was always convinced that kids could spend years trying to play a violin or other stringed instrument. Give them brass to play and they could play in an ensemble in weeks. I set up the SW16 Youth Brass Band with instruments collected from the defunct Hammersmith Band and recruited youngsters from the local primary school. We played our first gig about 3 months or so later. Sam, my eldest son was an early recruit and he still can't play the cornet. I suppose playing Bb bass with Yorkshire Imperial will have to do.

Some time later, in 1984 I moved to York. I started off commuting to York from London and sat in with the Railway Institute before opting for Rowntrees under Trevor Bousfield. The Band Committee was run by Ray Rochester. Trevor worked at the Tech during the day and must have slaved over his musical writing all night. He was a prodigious arranger and the Band is fortunate to have some 60 of his pieces in its library today. One regular gig for the Band in those days was dining-in night at RAF Linton.

By now I was back on 2nd cornet so could not see much of what went on that fateful night. The Band had been told that pilots from other countries, including Germany, were present at dinner. We thoughtfully included the Austrian Hymn in our program for them. To make up for that we also included, the RAF March, Magnificent Men, Dam Busters and Pomp and Circumstance. The effect was electrifying. Apparently more than £1,000 worth of damage was done to the chandelier. Rowntrees were asked to choose less provocative music for its subsequent engagements there. Howard Bousfield, Robert Melling, James Stockdale, John Wood, Neil and Gareth Overton – all fine musicians, came and went. From Dijon to Glasgow, Rowntrees was in seemingly endless demand. The opening of the Viking Centre with Prince Charles was one gig I missed. The commissioning of HMS York at Rosyth was one I did not. It was the first time that a civilian band had officiated at such a ceremony. There were civic dignitaries of all sorts. The Band had been bussed up to Scotland for the event but probably nobody really had a clue as to our actual location. We arrived at our hotel in the middle of the night. Once we'd played it was back on the bus and a return to York. Somewhere the Band has a commemorative plate presented to it by the ship's captain. Other memorable moments include the time when Rowntrees were fighting the Nestle takeover. The Band was sent to London by train one night ready to play the next morning on an open-topped bus as it toured through the City and on to the House of Commons. The company paid for us to stay at the Hilton in Park Lane. Big mistake that – especially for folk who'd never stayed in a hotel before. You actually have to pay for the minibar and room service. Still it was a great day out.

Conductors came and went. Chris Lawn – whose father, it turned out, had been with the Crystal Palace Band. Duncan Beckley – another top class band trainer who really gave Rowntrees it first taste of success at contesting. Derek Warley. Ray Farr. By now Trevor Collins was Chairman and work was still piling in. Pressure from my other musical interests – playing jazz piano with a six-piece outfit at Malton – led to a decision to cease banding. That must have been about 1992 or thereabouts. I occasionally played with Rowntrees for Area Contests. I even signed for Railway doing the same - 2nd baritone if I remember rightly. But brass bands and banding seemed behind me for good. One night I went back to the Rowntree Band Room to listen to the band. By now Sam was playing bass with the band. Chris Hurst was conducting. He asked me if I played cornet. When I said that I was a bass player I got taken on immediately – it was the usual story. Bass players are like rocking horse droppings in this part of the world. Under Chris we not only did well at area but went on to win the trophy for the best bass section (Yes !!). Rejoining Rowntrees was absolutely the right decision for me (the Band is welcome to its own opinion). It may be the same old soap opera but the music is great. For those outside banding they will probably not have a clue about the way brass bands change your life. I would not have missed a minute of it.

William Lane (Percussion) joined 2002

Back in 1995 I started towards learning the cornet but gave up in 1997 to learn percussion.

I progressed from there and my first ever brass band was Swinton and District whom I left to join Nestlé Rowntree Band, which I did 6 months ago. My dad has been a member of the band since 1999 and recently became the Principal cornet player.

I currently attend Ryedale School and at weekends I work on the nearby farm.

After learning percussion for about 3 years I bought my first drum kit. Through experience in banding, I have learnt to play a wide range of percussion – from timpani to tubular bells. My first concert was during 2002 – I enjoyed it very much.

Jennifer (Jenny) Lang (3rd Cornet) joined 2001

When I was 13 days old my parents moved from Scotland to York.

At 2 years of age I joined the York City Gymnastics Club and competed with the 'Squad' from the age of 4, winning several medals and a trophy.

In 1992 we moved to Saudi Arabia where I continued to do gymnastics and started to learn my first musical instrument – the descant recorder (when I was 7). My mum taught me and aged 10 I took my first music exam (ASBRM Grade 2) on the recorder. My mum started a recorder ensemble and I learned to play all 5 different recorders (at different times). I also began to learn the flute. Whilst in Riyadh, I played 2nd Flute and piccolo in the pit orchestra for a production of Gilbert and Sullivan's 'HMS Pinafore' – I was the youngest musician in the pit, by quite a number of years.

We returned to the UK in 1996 and I continued to play flute and piccolo, but gave up gymnastics. I started secondary school that year and took up the piano – gaining exam success in both traditional piano and jazz piano.

About 4 years ago I got my first horse, Jake, - I had been horse riding for several years. I only had Jake for 2 months as he bolted one day, when I was on him and I ended up spending the night in hospital with concussion. Shortly after that (having checked out lots of other horses) we got my current horse, Ginny, whom I've had for almost 4 years now.

I successfully completed 10 GCSE's at Easingwold School and I am currently studying (at Easingwold 6th Form) for A-levels in Psychology, Sociology and Home Economics (and General Studies). I have also got AS in these subjects (except General Studies) and also AS in Biology.

In the school orchestra I am principal, playing flute and piccolo, and also lead the school concert band, and I sing in the school choir performing a solo at the Christmas 2002 concert. The school concert band have been on 2 tours whilst I have been a member – we went to Paris and to Belgium.

In August 2000 I decided to start playing the cornet. I had gone along to so many of the senior band's concerts and contests, and also played with Bilsdale Silver Band and Thirsk Band, that I decided to join the Rowntree Junior Band. I played flugel for about 6 months before moving back onto cornet and to the repiano part. I have recently moved onto the solo cornet row and am really enjoying that. Last summer I played with the senior band a couple of times and was then asked to come along to senior band rehearsals where I now sit on 3rd cornet.

I have a part-time job at British Home Stores, in York, on the Customer Services Desk. I have worked there for the past 2 years and really enjoy my job and mixing with the other staff. I hope to be able to keep this job next year when I go to university. I am hoping to go to Durham University (Queens Campus, Stockton) and want to study Applied Psychology with the intention of eventually studying and practicing Clinical Psychology.

Sharon Lang (Solo Cornet 4) joined 1996

I was born in Paisley, Scotland, and have 1 brother and 1 sister.

The primary school I went to had several brass bands, as many schools did at that time. When I was 7 the bandmaster came into my class and asked all of us to smile. Those who had their 'new' front teeth were in the band. We were all asked our names – 'Anderson?' – he said to me, 'Doesn't your sister play in band?' (she did) – 'Right then, you're on the front row – play me a G'. That was Mr James (Jimmy) Colquhoun – the man was a legend in our area.

Two years later Mr Colquhoun invited me to join Barrhead Burgh Band (Junior Section) and later still I became Principal – I was the only girl in the junior section. When I was moved up to the Senior Band I was variously asked to play cornet, (left-handed) Flugel and finally Soprano.

I left and joined Johnstone Silver Band, where my sister (Irene) was, so that I could get back to playing Bb cornet and thoroughly enjoyed my time there. It was whilst with this band that I met my future husband, Andrew, who was the Solo Trombone player.

A few years after leaving school I decided to train to be a nurse and so left Johnstone to join Renfrew Burgh Band, on the back row of the cornet section, as I was unable to make regular rehearsals due to the shift work. I stopped playing when Andrew and I started our family and moved 'south of the border'.

Over the next 10 years I followed Andrew around the country and beyond, as he was an RAF pilot, and later a Flying Instructor both in the UK and lastly in Saudi Arabia (Riyadh). Whilst we were in Riyadh I took up playing again to help out at the school – they didn't have a brass teacher – but they did have a lot of pupils wanting to play brass instruments.

We were in Riyadh when there was a suicide bomb in the centre of the city, which killed several Americans. I was deeply honoured to be asked to play 'The Taps' (like our Last Post) at the Memorial Service, in front of hundreds of grieving friends and relatives, diplomats, military officials and members of the Saudi Royal family. This was without doubt the most difficult experience of my musical career.

We returned to the UK in 1996, and I joined Nestlé Rowntree Band shortly afterwards. I have loved my time with the band, (except for a short spell on Soprano) it is by far the friendliest band I have ever played in. My husband joined the band for a short time also, but unfortunately work commitments prevented him continuing – he is now an airline pilot with British Airways.

Last year, my daughter joined the band which has been a great treat for me.

Currently, I work as an Officer Manager (Finance Officer) at Ralph Butterfield Primary School in Haxby and I live in Shipton-by-Beningbrough with my husband, Andrew and our 2 children – Jenny and Christopher.

Mike Pratt (Solo Euphonium) joined 1991

I first became interested in learning a brass instrument around the age of 10/11.

The school I attended did not have the facilities for me to learn an instrument, but fortunately, both my mother, Grace, and my father, Ted, were excellent cornet and trumpet players – and my father was a peripatetic brass teacher in the York area. This was an obvious advantage and I started to learn the cornet. However, after a year or so of struggling to produce a sound reminiscent of a cow in labour, I was persuaded to change to a proper instrument – the euphonium.

With the help and encouragement of my family, I progressed to being Solo Euphonium with the Railway Institute Training Band and in 1975 I joined the senior band on baritone. Eventually, I attained the position of Solo Euphonium with the senior band and stayed there until 1990.

Whilst I was playing with the Railway Institute Band I was lucky enough to be asked to play on (and appear in) a couple of television programmes for Yorkshire Television. The most memorable ones were 'A Touch of Frost' and 'Emmerdale'. I also played the title music for the popular programme 'Cleggs People'.

Towards the end of 1990 I was invited to join the Yorkshire Imperial Band, in Leeds, on baritone and I enjoyed an extremely satisfying (and successful) year with them. We qualified from the Yorkshire Area Contest, played in the All England Masters, the British Open and also in the National Finals – in the Royal Albert Hall. However, at the end of 1991 I decided that, due to family commitments (my 2nd son having just been born) it would be better for me to play for a more local band and I am pleased to say that Rowntree Band offered me a position.

Since then I have thoroughly enjoyed playing with Nestlé Rowntree Band and being part of a professional, friendly, organisation, which (in achieving Championship status) has reaped the reward it deserves.

I currently work for a firm called Railpart UK Ltd, which is based in Doncaster, and (for my sins) I will complete 24 years working in the railway industry in October this year.

I am married to Heather (whom I met whilst playing with the Railway Institute Band) and we have 2 sons – Chris (13) and James (11). Chris has shown an interest in banding and is currently learning the euphonium and will, hopefully, follow me into the band just as I followed my parents.

To close, I would like to thank my father, Ted, who sadly died in 1997, for teaching, encouraging and supporting me through my banding career.

Dennis Stamp (First Horn) joined 1961

'Would you like to play a cornet?' -

That was the question asked by my dad at the age of 10. I said I did, knowing full well that it meant for life.

Mr Les Lambert, the then bandmaster of the Rowntree Cocoa Works Band, taught me at the Joseph Rowntree School and within 6 months had me sitting on the back row, with the band.

During my school days I progressed with my playing and was entered for solo competitions in the North of England. At the age of 13 I won my first competition at the Whitby Spa, playing a piece called 'I'll Walk Beside You'.

I come from a banding family, with my dad playing baritone, Ray (my eldest brother) playing cornet, Ken (brother) playing horn (now trombone), Pauline (sister) playing horn and Keith (brother) playing cornet. Most of my playing days were on Flugel Horn, but now playing 1st horn is about right for me. My daughter (Karen) and son (Paul) also played with the band, Karen played cornet and the Flugel Horn and Paul still plays cornet with the band.

In 1977 I left the band and joined the York Railway Institute Band, a 1st Section band – fast becoming a Championship Section band, in the Yorkshire area. I stayed with this band for approximately 14 years. In this time we made 2 L.P.'s and had several tours abroad and also made the finals in London on a number of occasions.

In 1992 I rejoined the Rowntree Band on Solo Horn. We were then in the 2nd Section, but after a number of hard working years, we have now, at this time, become a Championship Section Band, in the North East of England area.

At the present moment I work for Nestlé Rowntree, as an Electrician, and I am the only member of the Senior band working for the company.

In the early nineties, I formed the Beginners Band with about 20 members, some of which have now become Senior Band members.

Paul Stamp (2nd Cornet) joined 1991

I first started playing the cornet at the age of about 7, with the York Railway Institute (junior band). The conductor was Roy Waterhouse. My Granddad was playing with the York Railway Institute Golden Rail band, with my sister. My dad and 2 uncles were playing with the York Railway Institute (senior band). Monday's were rehearsal night.

During this time I met Sharon Greenfield (now Fallon), Mike Pratt, Mark Durham and Andrew Durham – these are now members of Nestlé Rowntree Band.

Roy Waterhouse was a real character and I owe him a great deal for putting up with me as a youngster – this must have been really difficult. To this day Sharon Greenfield and I still remember him slapping the stool he used to have, and watching the dust emerge. Newer members turned increasingly white. I used to write a diary around this time and one Monday reads: 'been off school with flu, went to dentist for two teeth out. Tonight I went to band'.

After a few years, at around the age of eleven, I joined the York Railway Institute Golden Rail Band, conducted by John Warley. I remember doing my very first area competition. I played the repiano part on the piece 'Four Fours for Brass' – we didn't win. I can also remember doing my first band job, it was at the Citadel on Gillygate in York. I played 3rd cornet next to my Granddad. During this time we seemed to do endless band jobs through the summer months. I stayed with the Golden Rail Band until I was around 14 before sitting in with the Senior Band.

My dad and two uncles were playing in the senior band, the conductor was Barry Thomson – I was at a stage where I would sit in and rehearse on 3rd cornet, but my banding came to an end (at the York Railway Institute) when various senior members on the committee decided that they did not want to introduce youngsters who had come through their junior bands into the senior band. At this stage, my dad decided that it was time to move on and hopefully join a band that would bring me on as a player.

In 1991 we joined Rowntree Band, conducted by Derek Warley, son of John Warley's (Golden Rail Band). Around this time Mike Pratt had joined the band and we were in the Second section.

About a year after joining, I was given the opportunity to play the Flugel horn, which is the position I held with the band until 1997. In 1992 and 1993 we qualified for the National Finals in London, and in 1993 and 1995 made visits to the Ballerup Festival, Copenhagen. I also recorded the Flugel Horn solo 'Concerto de Aranjuez' on the band's debut CD. The CD was recorded with our, then, new conductor Chris Hirst, who is now my brother-in-law.

In 1998, I joined the Rothwell Temperance Band, conducted by David Roberts. The band was in the First section when I joined them – that year the band qualified for the First section National Finals, in Nottingham. We played a piece called 'Midsummer Sonata' and I did many jobs throughout the year. Although I enjoyed my time at Rothwell, it was becoming increasingly difficult to travel there, financially; my working hours had also changed, leaving me with no option but to leave the band.

I am now back playing with Nestlé Rowntree Band, I am 25 years old and work as a printer in York. Thanks to the last 10 years of hard work we are in the Championship section.

The band also has a Beginner's band, which was started by my dad (circa 1994), which I was involved in. With the addition of the Concert band (and the Senior band as well) we hopefully have the backbone for another one hundred years.

Cath Tobitt (2nd Euphonium) joined 2001

I've been musical from an early age. My mum walked into the room to hear me playing a tune on my toy xylophone, that I'd just heard on the TV.

At primary school I began playing the recorder and, at the age of 11, the cornet. (My great uncle Charlie played for Brighouse and Rastrick, so I guess to some extent, banding is in the blood!) I very quickly joined the local junior band, Clifton & Lightcliffe where I progressed, via Tenor Horn, onto euphonium and decided this was the instrument I wanted to play. I also played for Emley band for a few years, during my early teens.

At the age of 16 I began my 'A' level courses in music and French, at Huddersfield Technical College, School of Music, where I had euphonium lessons from Nick Childs and played in bands conducted by Phillip McCann and Major Peter Parkes. I joined Warren band, based at Huddersfield and conducted by Duncan Beckley (who was later to become a conductor at Rowntree Band). Warren were big rivals with Phillip McCann's own band (Tecol) – who later became Sellers Engineering. Many of my college friends played for Tecol and had spent most of the term telling me how much better they were than us. So, it was somewhat satisfying when we beat them in the National Finals in 1986.

Around this time I was also playing for the Northern Youth Brass which was a very successful youth band, winning many competitions and giving me my first opportunity to play at the Royal Albert Hall. I think it's a shame that the lower section National Finals are no longer held in London. It used to be a real occasion and it just doesn't have the same ring to it saying 'we've qualified to go to Harrogate' (or wherever) – sorry, Harrogate!!

I went away to college in Ripon in 1987 to study for an honours degree in music and French. I continued playing at Warren when I could, but by then the band was struggling for players and eventually folded. I played for Tingley band for a while also, and then in my final year at Ripon, I joined Barrow Band (now Barnsley Building Society).

Whilst at university, I lived in Grenoble, France, for 4 months and studied music there at the Conservatoire de Musique, with all the French students. Whilst there, I had to give a talk all about the euphonium (in French!) to all my fellow students. In my final year at Ripon I completed my special study – a 10,000 word dissertation on the euphonium. This involved writing to composers, instrument manufacturers and players to research the subject. I also taught myself to play the trombone at college. The swing band was, by far, the best band there, but they didn't want a euphonium player, so I just had to learn trombone.

I moved to Barnsley and did my post-graduate teaching certificate at Bretton Hall College, Wakefield. Despite the experience of having a gunman in school whilst on my teaching practice, I completed the course and qualified to teach secondary school music. My first post was teaching at Grimethorpe, an area renowned for it's world-famous brass band. After a couple of years I moved back to Bradford to take up a new teaching post. I then played at Yorkshire Co-operatives (better known as Jayess) where my husband is still a member, followed by a brief stint back at Tingley, as one of my friends was playing there at the time. He's also a euphonium player, and together we had a real laugh. I think we were as infamous for our mad sense of humour as our playing abilities! He then got a job as a paramedic with unpredictable shifts, so he had to leave.

It wasn't so much fun without him, so I then went to play for Stocksbridge (just missing out on their film debut in 'The Full Monty'). When I left Stocksbridge, I decided that, having played in a band for almost 20 years without a break, I'd have some time out. I managed a full weekend before I was approached to join Drighlington. It was here that I met Billy, Nestlé Rowntree Band's current conductor. When he left Drighlington, he asked me to go and do the area contest with Nestlé Rowntree Band.

When I went to the first rehearsal it struck me how friendly the band was. I was only supposed to be helping out, but I'm still here 2 years on and still enjoying the great atmosphere this band has.

Charles Wilson (2nd Horn) joined 1987

As I write this, I am 39 years old and have been playing for 16 years. Currently, I am on tenor horn, I say currently as over the years I have had a catholic view to playing in the band.

When I first joined, I was playing 3rd man down on the front row (cornet). After 2 years I moved to bumper up (Solo Cornet 2). From there I felt my talents would better be suited to the back row of the cornet section and I moved onto the infamous Soprano cornet. This unhappy marriage lasted a year until the band found somebody who could actually play it. I returned to the front row (SC 2) and ended up as Principal for about 9 months – whilst the band sorted out a full time replacement.

In 1995, I felt that I had been missing all the fun and exploits of the back row so I moved, again, this time to repiano and over the next 3 years I slowly slid down the row via 2nd cornet to 3rd.

Having explored every nook and cranny of the cornet section I became aware that Solo Baritone was beckoning me and I spent a pleasant 18 months there, before new blood arrived and I moved to 2nd Baritone. That all ended shortly afterwards as the back row of the cornet section again needed a 3rd cornet, I once again traversed the bandroom and became ensconced on familiar ground.

That is probably where I would have been today, however, there was a niche in the horn section (1st Horn) which needed to be filled, and in I went. Again, when new talent arrived I moved aside (2nd Horn) where you can find me today – in my niche, at the centre of it all, in the middle of the band...

Alongside my playing career, I have always taken a healthy interest in running the band (having held every position on the committee and one time or another – and even waggling the stick on the odd occasion, when the conductor was on holiday). My longest held position, on the committee, was that of chairman from 1995 – 1999 when due to work commitments I had to relinquish the position. For my sins I have taken the position again and am currently the acting chairman until some other poor unsuspecting soul takes up the challenge.

Most of my playing career has been with Rowntree Band and I have seen a number of changes over the years – some good and some not so. I actually started playing when I was 13, at school, and quickly joined Easingwold Town Band. The band flourished for a good few years and then started to wither in the 1980's, due to the loss of some players and changes in conductors.

Whilst at university I played with Brancepeth and Willington Welfare Band, a good old fashioned, traditional mining band – without the mine. This was a seriously good time and it was quite a good band as well. By the time I returned to Easingwold, after college, it didn't appear as though the band was going anywhere and the standard had dropped quite a bit. Even with me taking over and running the band, and doing some teaching, the writing was on the wall.

I was approached by Howard Bousfield, in May 1987, to come and play with Rowntree Band for that year's National Finals in London. It only took 2 rehearsals for me to make the move permanent. Since then, I have been lucky enough to compete in a further 5 National Finals, with Nestlé Rowntree Band.

I moved house from Easingwold to Huddersfield in 1999, but still travel twice a week for rehearsal with the band which has been such a large part of my life.

One of my driving aims has been to see the band reach Championship status, something it had been threatening to do for a number of years. This dream was finally realised in 2001 with our promotion to the Championship section. Another major milestone is the centenary celebrations, something of an honour, as I will certainly not see the next one. My fervent hope is that in another hundred years the then members of the band, whatever it is called, will look back at these notes and feel a true sense of belonging, in the same way we have by looking back on the bands records from 1903.

SECTION 2

Behind the Stand

Concert Band

Audrey Brown - Conductor, Concert Band & Beginner's Band, 1988 to present day

I grew up in Micklefield, a pit village in West Yorkshire. There was a Brass Band in the village. I remember when I was young, seeing the Band marching and playing and wishing I could join, but the Band was for men and boys only, so instead I learnt the Piano. My Grandad was a very good singer and as soon as I became proficient on the piano he encouraged me to play while he sang. Later I played the organ at Church for services and then I took over accompanying the village Male Voice Choir. That was a lot of fun! With the Male Voice Choir I used to go to an Annual event at Sheffield for all the Coal Field Choirs and Brass Bands. It was fascinating watching famous conductors rehearsing the massed choirs and getting wonderful performances from them.

I left home for Teacher Training College and joined the Music Society there. That involved trips to Nottingham University for various musical performances with choirs from the surrounding area.

When I married Mick and moved to York our home was full of music, mainly Jazz and it wasn't until our daughter wanted to learn cornet and join a Brass Band that my early ambitions came to be realised. We joined Ebor Brass in York, one daughter on Cornet, Mick on Cornet, another daughter on Euphonium and myself on Baritone. From time to time we also persuaded our son to play percussion for us but he was really only interested in guitars.

After a few years our daughters left and a friend from my village asked us to help him resurrect the village Band, which had folded in the intervening years. We enjoyed this as rehearsals were at the village public house. However, after a time I found it very frustrating as the standard was low and nobody seemed to want to get better. Mick and I had gone on various music holidays and experienced playing with keen musicians and brilliant conductors. Now I wanted to play a better standard of music.

In the Autumn of 1988 as a favour to a friend we went to play with St. John's College Wind Band. Duncan Beckley conducted this band and also Rowntrees Band and he asked us to attend some rehearsals with Rowntrees. After a couple of rehearsals, Mick and I were taken into the Back Room by the committee and invited to sign up with the Band. It was like a dream come true to play with a band of ambitious musicians. Our first concert was in York Minster. What a magnificent experience playing with a good band in such great surroundings. The first contest we were involved in was the Durham League where we played "Resurgam" by Eric Ball.

Duncan Beckley departed and we had a succession of conductors over the next few years. All this time I was observing the conductors we played for and remembering my teacher training and contrasting their approach to other conductors I had seen, I would get ideas about how to conduct myself.

In 1992 I took over as Secretary and we won the Area Contest two weeks later, so my first job was to organise our trip to Wembley Conference Centre for the

Finals. We had a great time and managed to get in the frame. When we won again the following year at the Area Contest I thought it would be much easier to organise the trip to London, but I did not count on getting a Bus Driver who did not want to follow my instructions. We ended up at the Albert Hall instead of Wembley Conference Centre! Fortunately a late draw meant we had time to get to the correct venue.

In 1996 I retired from the Senior Band and went along to help the Training Band. The Beginners Band needed a conductor, so I volunteered. I was so nervous at the first rehearsal but I did enjoy it and then later I took over as conductor for the Training Band. I have tried to improve the quality of playing in both bands. I think sound is everything in the Beginners so I try to cultivate a good sound. It is great when someone new joins the band and within a few weeks they can play a simple tune with a good sound. I try to make sure our rehearsals are enjoyable, as I want our young players' first impressions to be pleasant.

Rehearsals with the Training Band, now named The Concert Band are more demanding. I still like it to be enjoyable, but also expect players to concentrate in the rehearsal and practice at home so that the standard can continue to rise. These exacting standards mean we have lost a few players, but that is unfortunate. I hope that they return to the Band in time with renewed enthusiasm.

My ambition now is to see lots of players who started with the Beginners Band move up through the Concert Band to the Seniors. Then I hope to see them on the stage at the Albert Hall contesting with the Senior Band for the Brass Band Championship of Great Britain. I am sure there are already players among the Beginners and Concert Band who are capable of doing this if they maintain the interest they show at present. I look forward to seeing them make their mark at the higher levels of banding.

Bruce Adamson (1st Baritone) joined 1999

During my early life I have played Piano, violin, guitar and flute. My involvement in playing brass bands began in 1983, when I was presented with a Euphonium and invited to play with a York Band called Ebor Brass. I played with the band until 1987 at which time my job in York was relocated to Teeside.

When approaching early retirement, I was asked if I would like to take up playing once again in 1999. Since this time I have been playing Baritone with the Rowntree Concert Band, which has been a very happy time.

Sean Aylett (Percussion) joined 1996

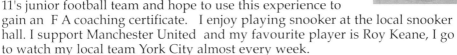

I am 16 years old and I have played in the band for 6 years having started on the trombone . I now play the drums in the concert band as well as playing in a band of my own.

In my spare time I play football for a local team called Huntington. I also play football for school. I coach an under 11's junior football team and hope to use this experience to gain an F A coaching certificate. I enjoy playing snooker at the local snooker hall. I support Manchester United and my favourite player is Roy Keane, I go to watch my local team York City almost every week.

I like listening to rock music, my favourite band is the Red Hot Chilli Peppers.

I attend Huntington School and I am studying for 11 GCSE's. My favourite subjects are Geography and English. I will hopefully be staying on at school to do my A-levels.

Thomas Aylett (Eb Bass) joined 1996

I play an Eb bass instrument for the Concert Band and also help with the Beginner's Band. When I first joined the band I used to play a trombone but soon moved onto the Eb Bass.

I am married with 2 teenage boy's. My eldest son plays the drums in the band and my younger son used to play a cornet. I became interested in playing an instrument when taking my sons to the band once a week.

After spending 15 years working as a Mining Contractor on the Selby Coalfields, I now work for Royal Mail as a Postman. I hold an FA Coaching Certificate which I put to use running a football team in Huntington, which my son is a member of.

Matthew Breslin (Solo Cornet) joined circa 1999

I started learning cornet with the Railway Institute in 1997, when I was 7 years old. Shortly afterwards I moved to Rowntree Beginner's Band and I am now one of the solo cornets with the Concert Band which I joined about 3 years ago.

I am in my second year at Joseph Rowntree School and play in the swing band, after school. At home I have a drum kit which I love to play and also a didgeridoo, which I am learning!!

I also play the djembe with the Trans-Global Drummers, we are a young drumming phenomenon who play multi-ethnic music. We are hoping to go to Ghana next year to learn more about their music.

None of my family are very musical, but my great-grandad played the drums when he was stationed in India, with the West Yorkshire Regiment.

I am taking music grades in cornet, piano and drums this year and hope to carry on with music when I leave school – perhaps as a musical technician or some similar kind of role.

Mick Brown (Solo Cornet) joined 1988

I first started to play a brass instrument when I was 18 years old. I had previously done 2 years of piano lessons, but gave that up when I discovered Louis Armstrong and jazz.

I had seen an advertisement in the 'Melody maker' and bought an old cornet for £10 on easy payments. I bought myself a tutor and taught myself the fingering. The music side was easy because of the piano playing experience.

I started a New Orleans style Jazz Band with some fellow enthusiasts and started doing gigs. We called ourselves 'The San Jacinto Jazz Band'. The band continued playing for about 2 years and after that I started playing piano again with a modern style band.

I was now listening to, and trying to play like, great pianists such as Earl Hines, Art Tatum, Teddy Wilson and Oscar Peterson. We used to rehearse in 'The Black Swan' in Peasholme Green. Eventually this jazz group was taken over by a prominent York dance band leader – Johnny Sutton. He was a trumpet player who learned to play with Rowntree Cocoa Works Band. Johnny's brother was Ted Sutton, who was Principal cornet with the Cocoa Works Band.

This new dance band was called 'The J.R. Big Sound' after the bandleaders name (J.R. Sutton) and played for dancing in Scarborough Spa, Bridlington Spa and York and District.

I took up playing a cornet again, many years later, when my 2 daughters were having cornet lessons. The man who was teaching them said he was starting his own brass band and asked them to join. The girls told him that their dad used to play trumpet and so I was asked to join. That was how I became a founder member of Ebor Brass. Through this I discovered the wonderful world of brass bands and some of the great music and musicians within it.

When I joined Rowntree Brass Band in 1988 the conductor was Duncan Beckley and they were Third Section Champions and had been promoted to Second Section. The first contest I played with them the test piece was Eric Ball's 'Resurgam'. I thought that we had played well enough to be in the frame, but I think we finished in 6th place. That piece is so moving that I shall never forget that performance.

I left some years later to play with another jazz group on piano, and returned when the then Training Band was desperately in need of players following the death of Ted Pratt.

Tim Clark (Solo Horn) joined 1997

I was first introduced to the brass band world by my son, Andrew, who plays cornet in the Senior Band. He encouraged me to learn to play a brass instrument, at the tender age of 44. Before then, I had never played any musical instrument, and could not even read music.

After a painful few weeks, I joined the Beginner's Band. I can remember bravely entering the slow melody contest, playing 'Abide with Me', and getting a tremendous round of applause. I was extremely proud of myself! I eventually progressed to the Training Band (now called the Concert Band), where I now play Solo Horn.

I am married to Liz, who gave me my tenor horn as a silver wedding present. I also have a daughter, Nicola, and live in Haxby. I now work for the County Council, managing the training unit of the Social Services Directorate. Between 1975 and 1991 I worked for Rowntree Mackintosh. Both my father (Ian) and grandfather (Jack) worked for the company. My brother (Chris), who sadly died in 2000, also worked for Rowntree's at the Fawdon factory.

I attended Archbishop Holgate's Grammar School and went to the University of Newcastle-upon-Tyne. Apart from my university years, I have always lived in the York area.

David Gregg (2nd Trombone) joined 1991

My son, Daniel, was a member of the Beginner's Band from 1988 and I was the taxi to concerts and rehearsals.

Even though I had no previous musical experience, I thought that I would like to take part. I bought a cheap trombone and had lessons from the fantastic Ted Pratt. I was soon playing in the Beginner's Band and, after about 3 years, occasionally sat in at concerts with the Senior Band, playing with my son Daniel – who now plays front row Cornet with the Westoe Band.

I now play regularly with the Concert Band and am thoroughly enjoying the music (well, most of it anyway!). I particularly enjoy playing rousing marches and music that has a 'good tune', whether it is pop or classical.

I do not consider myself a good player and I am certainly not dedicated, or good enough, to play with the Seniors, but I am still improving as time goes by. I look forward to playing in concerts, especially those where there are larger audiences and have nice settings.

I also help Audrey Brown by producing the engagement lists, keeping the band details and general photocopying.

Kathryn Holmes (2nd Horn) joined 2000

Whilst walking round a fete in the summer of 1999, a brass band was playing and I though how nice it would be to be able to be part of that.

I spoke to a band member (it was the Golden Rail band) and he said to come along and learn. So, at the end of 1999, I turned up to a rehearsal with no previous knowledge; they had a spare tenor horn, so that's what I tried to learn. After a couple of months I moved to Nestlé Rowntree Beginner's Band and a year later joined the Training (Concert) Band, which was a steep learning curve!

I am a York person and I attended Queen Anne School, back when it was an all girls grammar, and have always worked full time, first for British Telecom and now for Coverdales Opticians. My previous hobbies have included being a chorus member of York Amateur Operatic Society and also tap dancing. I live in York with my partner Rod and our Welsh terrier, Holly.

As I never learned an instrument as a child, I am very slow at sight-reading, but have only met help and encouragement from Audrey and the other band members. Sharon Lang very kindly gave me some tuition and theory help and I try to practice as much as possible.

Unusually, I have no family connection with brass bands. My late father, John Holmes, worked for Rowntree's for over 30 years until his retirement in 1984. Unfortunately, he didn't live to see me in the Rowntree band, but I am sure it would have pleased him.

So, now I am able to go along and take part in the concerts as I originally wanted to do. I have a lot to learn, but it is so enjoyable, I look forward to continuing in the band.

Patrick Hubble (Solo Euphonium) joined 2002

I first learned to play on the trumpet, but soon switched over to the trombone and the euphonium.

I played in the Southampton Youth Band and Southampton Youth Orchestra when I was at school (1979 – 1984) and at university for the University of London Orchestra (1984 – 1986). After that, with a (not so useful) degree in Philosophy and family commitments, the trombone and euphonium both found their way into the loft.

I trained to be a lawyer in Leicester and practised as a solicitor in Middlesbrough. We moved to York in 2000 – now a family of five (plus Rhodesian Ridgeback), where I work at the College of Law (down Bishopthorpe Road from the Terry's factory).

When my son Sean first joined the Beginners Band at Rowntree, I dusted off the euphonium, after a 15 year gap, and started playing again. The fingers have not forgotten what to do, but the lip is not yet up to scratch! As Sean moved onto the Concert Band, so did I, and I'm very glad to be back playing regularly again.

Sean Hubble (2nd Cornet) joined 2002

I am 9 years old and was born in Middlesbrough.

I moved to York about 3 years ago and live in Otterwood Lane (but I still support Middlesbrough FC – as you can see in the picture, I am wearing one of their football shirts).

I hope Middlesbrough are still in the Premier League as you are reading this. My favourite player is Juninho.

I first started learning the trumpet at school with my friends. I learned to play on my uncle's old Vincent Bach trumpet, which is about 40 years old now! After about 6 months I joined Rowntree Beginner's Band and after another 6 months I joined the Concert Band. At band I play on the band's cornet and at the moment I am a 2nd cornet player. Last year's Christmas concert was the first concert which I've played in.

I go to English Martyr's School in Hamilton Drive, Holgate, which I think is a good school. My teacher is called Mr Mulkeen. My friends are Liam, Andrew, Brian and James. My other interests are cricket and football.

In the summer I play cricket for Ovington cricket Club Under 10's, for the rest of the year I play football for Hamilton panthers Under 10's – both of these play opposite the Knavesmire.

David Maddison (2nd Baritone) joined 2000

I was born in York, 3rd May, 1944, the son of Harold and Gladys Maddison.

My father played many instruments, including cornet, harmonica, recorder and mandolin, and for a period he played with the Railway Institute Band. My mother played piano and church organ for Sunday School (at St. Aidan's Church, Acomb).

Unfortunately, I showed no real aptitude for any musical instruments, although whilst attending St Barnabas School I did join the St Barnabas Church Choir (aged 9) for a couple of years. When we moved to Acomb, in 1954, attendance became difficult. I attended Westfield School, Acomb, for a couple of years (along with my sister Renee) re-attempting the recorder whilst there.

At the age of 11 I started Acomb Secondary Modern School (now Oaklands) and continued with the recorder, and for a period joined the Harmonica Club (with only moderate success). My favourite subjects at school were woodwork and metalwork. Musically, singing was my main interest. My music mistress (Miss Herman) was very keen on Spanish music, and was always playing recordings obtained on annual holidays in Spain.

I joined the Scout movement in November, 1955, in Holgate (1st York St. Pauls Group) – the oldest troup in York (established on 22nd February, 1909 – also Baden Powell's birthday). I worked my way up through the ranks to Patrol leader in 1958. One of the highlights of that years was winning (with a team of 6) the York and District 'Scoutcraft Competition'. Camping, for me, became the most enjoyable part of scouting, we visited North Wales, the Lake District, Scotland and many parts of North Yorkshire.

At 16 I went on to become Cub Scout Leader for a period of 10 years. The group eventually moved out to Poppleton, following a decline in the number of youngsters in the Holgate area.

I started work as an apprentice watchmaker in 1959, for a city centre jewellers, learning to repair jewellery, clocks and finally watches. Strange as I have always wanted to become a joiner/cabinet maker. At the age of 20 I left to become self-employed, working in several different locations in York – Walmgate; Bootham; Coppergate and finally, in 1971, in Colliergate – dealing with watch sales and repairs.

I married my wife, Rita, in 1970, at the church in Shipton-by- Beningbrough, and we have lived in a couple of different locations in York before finally settling in Heworth, in 1982. During the late 70's I enjoyed, over a 5 year period, playing folk and then classical guitar at evening classes. This, if nothing else, gave me a wider appreciate of different musical styles and the discovery of many new composers.

My main interest during the 80's and 90's became running, I joined Rowntree Athletics Club and started racing, doing endless 10k, marathons, fell racing (including the 3 peaks race 10 times) and climbing in the Western Highlands and Islands of Scotland. The climax of my racing days was to do the London Marathon, 1991, in 2 hrs and 44 mins (my personal best).

As the years rolled by, old age and injuries played an ever increasing part of my life's tapestry – the approaching 'New Millennium' suggested that a new challenge might be appropriate – to mark the occasion.

My run training nights were the same as brass band practice and I had become familiar with some members of the band and was finally persuaded, by Roger's mum (cornet player) to join the Beginner's Band, on a Monday night. Eventually I moved to the Training Band on Wednesday's and although, not always easy, I have found it to be a very rewarding and enjoyable experience.

Richard Merchant (Cornet) joined 1996

I began playing with Rowntrees in 1996 whilst having lessons with, the then conductor Ted Pratt. I had previously had lessons at Fulford Primary School through the music company 'Normans' and started playing in 1994. Over the years in Rowntrees I have played 3rd Cornet, 2nd Cornet, Repiano, Flugel, Horn and currently Solo Cornet. I have seen many members, conductors and even names of the band come a go over the past 7 years, but I have remained.

I currently attend Fulford Comprehensive 6th Form, studying Chemistry, Physics, Maths and DT for my AS Levels, and hope to go on to University to study Product Design.

Richard Peacock (Repiano Cornet) joined 1999

I joined the band about four years ago when I was told about it from friend. I was going to join the school band, but this sounded better   !

I started in absolute beginners because I didn't know anything about playing a cornet, then I went into beginners a year later. I have worked my way up to the Concert Band, with lots of practise, and I now play repiano. I love going to band and I now play in the school jazz band occasionally.

The reason I love playing in the band so much is because one of my great granddads used to play in Rowntrees band and my granddad loved brass band and military music.

I go the Millthorpe School and I am in Year 9. I have just chosen my options for GCSE. I have chosen to do resistant materials because I love working with wood and would one day like to be a joiner or a professional wood turner.

I have made lots of new friends going to band, I enjoy taking part in concerts and going to different places to play all the different music we learn.

Janet Phillips (2nd Horn) joined 1995

I first joined the Beginner's Band in 1995, shortly after my youngest daughter, Ruth, and my niece, Olivia Evans, had started to learn the cornet. (Olivia's dad, Mick, was playing tenor horn with the Senior Band.)

I was 'volunteered', rather than being a 'volunteer', thanks to Dennis Stamp (who was the founder/conductor of the Beginner's Band).

I was widowed the following year, so having an outside interest has been very important to me. My brother-in-law, Mick Evans, my sister, Gill, and I follow the Senior Band with great interest. We even went to Denmark when Mick was a member of the Seniors, and still have the friends we made there, from the Baldur Band.

I'm not convinced that I'll ever make the Senior Band, but I'll keep on practising and enjoying the music I do play.

I was 42 when I started to play and instrument – and couldn't read a note of music – so you're never too old to start!

Sam(antha) Scott (Flugel Horn) joined 2002

I am new to the world of brass banding, and was initially attracted to the band by the warm welcome I received, but am starting to see what I have been missing musically. Previously I had only ever played in Concert Bands or the school orchestra.

I came to York in 1999, to take up a job in the university's computing department. Once I had completed my part-time degree studies, in 2001, I decided it was time to get out and meet people and what better way than through music.

I still play with the Symphonic Concert Band, in my old home town – Shipley (West Yorkshire) – but the brass band has fast become my second love.

Don Simpson (Solo Trombone) joined 1999

When I was at Nunthorpe Grammar School, from 1949 to 1954, the weekly music lesson was pretty poor. The only instrument I ever saw at school was a piano.

Since leaving school, I've been a jazz lover and at about 18 years old I really fancied a trombone (inspired by Kid Ory, Vic Dickenson, etc). Lack of finance dictated otherwise, although I did manage to 'play' tea-chest bass in a post-school jazz band.

Real music hit me in 1978 when I was 40 and joined Bilsdale Silver Band, as a complete novice, on a circa 1900 'peashooter' trombone. Bilsdale had been defunct for nearly a year when Dick Blackford took over as conductor. He realised that I had a company car and free petrol from Tetley's Brewery, so a symbiotic situation arose and we were able to reinforce Bilsdale's 7 or 8 members with help from York at no cost. With these extra bodies the band survived.

In the early 80's I also played for Ebor Brass and, for a short time after that, Micklefield Band.

I was made redundant in 1987 by Tetleys and became a self-employed Chartered Quantity Surveyor. Opportunities for practising and playing diminished over the next few years as work took over.

It was only after retirement in 1999 that playing again became a possibility, with Bilsdale. Then Audrey and Mick Brown, who had been friends for 20 years or more, suggested that I came down to the Training (Concert) band. I've really enjoyed playing with the Concert Band and, having at last bought a new Yamaha trombone, am looking forward to playing here and at Bilsdale for many years to come.

Ian Smith (Repiano Cornet) joined 2002

I was born in York on 21st April, 1956, and attended Tanghall Junior School and then Burnholme Secondary Modern School.

My musical career began when I was 11 years old, learning to play the cornet with the York Railway Insitute Junior Band. My first public engagement was in the summer of 1968, on the village green at Nun Monkton Fayre. A year later I progressed into the senior band playing 3rd then 2nd cornet. Among the solo cornet players at that time were Ted and Grace Pratt, parents of Mike Pratt, who now plays in the Nestlé Rowntree Band (Seniors).

At this time I had my first experiences of contesting, regional ones at first: Ryedale (won); York (won); Leeds (won) then onto the National Finals in London in 1970 and again in 1971. We were up against some of the bigger names in brass band circles.

I gave up playing the cornet when I was 16 and decided to play the bass guitar in a rock band instead, playing in pubs and clubs around York and parts of Yorkshire. I did this for a number of years until hanging up my guitar in the late 80's. I wasn't until my eldest daughter took up playing the saxophone, in her school big band a couple of years ago, that I felt inspired (after 28 years) to pick up the cornet again. I briefly rejoined the Railway Institute Golden Rail Band in January, 2002, playing 2nd cornet again.

In September, 2002, I saw the Rowntree Training Band perform on the bandstand at Wetherby and was impressed by the quality of musical material and standard of playing. I made a few enquiries to Audrey and was invited to join, initially on 2nd cornet but now playing repiano. I enjoy the challenge although some of the higher notes leave me somewhat breathless as I never used to have to play that high.

I am currently employed at Sessions of York, the Quaker family printing company where I served my apprenticeship, and am now Foreman of the Commercial Print Division. I am married to Jackie and have 2 children, Emily - born 1989 and Rebecca – born 1991. My musical preferences range from the Beatles to Led Zeppelin, Dave Brubeck to Jimi Hendrix, and last but certainly not least – the great Glenn Miller. I hope to continue playing for many years to come.

Richard Smith (Solo Cornet) joined 1997

Life begins at 40, or so they say. Well, I am here to tell you that all sorts of strange things can begin at 40.

For me, playing in a brass band began at 40. I am one of several players in the Concert Band who started playing, relatively late in life, when one of their children started. My daughter, Kirsten, took up the trumpet and so did I, to keep her company – so to speak.

When I decided to join a band and came along to Rowntree, she came too, even though she already played in several bands, to keep me company. I'm sure she thought I'd never cope alone.

We swopped our trumpets for cornets and for a while we progressed together, but she has long ago left me far behind. If I can be forgiven for misquoting P.G. Woodhouse 'brass playing, like golf and measles, should be caught young'.

At school, I played the violin, and then the viola, in the orchestra and I enjoyed that, but all I can say is it's not like the real thing! The obvious advantage of playing in a band is that, musically, you are a small part of something bigger than each individual (and it's so much louder!). There is more to it than that though, many of the band are experienced players, and there is always something to learn from them. Thanks, Guys.

Fred Spencer (Percussion) joined 1994

Firstly, I brought my grandson to the Beginner's Band, as I so wanted him to play a musical instrument. Soon I was tapping out the rhythm on the unmanned timpani. My grandson and I move into the then 'Training band' and he stuck at it until senior school homework made attending band impossible

I was a bit of a pianist, but excelled with a knife and fork – drumming on a dinner plate – and my ability to read music helped considerably. I took a few lessons at the University Music Department and grew to be really fond of these great beasts (timpani) except when they were to be loaded into my tiny car en route to a concert venue.

I am getting older (really old) but the band seems to put up with my spirited, but less than perfect, playing. I have watched from the back and seen the newly named Concert Band grow, under the direction of Audrey Brown, into a strong and talented group. Long may it prosper.

Jacqui Tesselment (2nd Euphonium) joined 2000

I started learning the trumpet at school, at the age of 11.

After several months I was persuaded to try the tuba, as it had a bigger mouthpiece which would suit me better, apparently. Later I found out that they needed a tuba player for the school orchestra!

I played the tuba throughout school and in various groups such as Herfordshire County Youth Wind Orchestra. I took my Grade 8 at 18 and against all the odds was awarded a Distinction. (The examiner was a pianist who felt sorry for a girl playing the tuba!)

At university in Sheffield, despite the best of intentions, I only played a handful of times, but the tuba made a fine towel stand.

My first job at York University brought me into contact with Audrey Brown and I started playing, on an informal basis, with the Seniors. After a year I moved to Loughborough University for a masters and took advantage of the free lessons on offer.

Whilst there, I helped out my brass teacher, playing with his school band at Twickenham for the rugby under 18 final (the march onto the pitch was woeful and the National Anthem little better). A few years in London put the tuba into retirement, but a final move back to York reunited me with the brass band once again.

After a year or so I needed a new challenge and took up the euphonium which I have been playing every since. It's great to play the tune occasionally!

I work at the University of York in Community Affairs. I enjoy walking, cycling and running in my spare time and attend St Oswald's Church.

SECTION 2

Behind the Stand

Beginner's Band

Amy Buck (Trombone) joined 2001

I joined the Beginner's Band in summer, 2001 and started to play the cornet, but now I play the trombone.

I attend Woodthorpe School. My likes are dance, karate and swimming. I dance on a Saturday at ballroom dancing and have 1 trophy. I have been doing karate for 4 months and have gained an orange belt. I am currently at level 6 in swimming.

I have played at 2 Christmas Concerts now, 2001 and 2002.

Chloe Buck (Tenor Horn) joined 2002

I'm learning the tenor horn and know a few notes.

I've had problems as I only have one hand, also, I'm only 5 years old. I go to Woodthorpe School. My likes are swimming and I have got up to level 5. I played the bells in the Christmas Concert, 2002.

Ryan Buck (Cornet) joined 2001

I joined the Beginner's Band in the summer, 2001. I started to play the cornet and am having lessons with Sharon Lang.

I attend Woodthorpe School. I like playing football and play for my school and for Dunnington under 10's – we are doing well. I also like karate, I have been doing that for 10 months and have reached a purple belt.

My mum and sisters also play in the Beginner's band and I have played in 2 Christmas Concerts – 2001 and 2002.

Jenine Buck (Cornet) joined 2002

I joined the Beginner's Band in the summer, 2002. I had been bringing my children along and sitting around waiting for them.

First of all I started to play the euphonium, until Christmas, 2002, then had to change onto cornet, and start all over again. I have 3 children (Ryan, Amy and Chloe) and we are expecting our fourth child in June, 2003.

I work for York City Council, part-time, as a crèche worker. I used to be a coach for York City Girls Football, but I had to give it up when Ryan took up his interest in football. I still keep fit by running around after the children and taking 2 dogs out for very long walks.

Andrew Metcalfe (Euphonium) joined 2003

I have been coming to the Beginners Band for four weeks now and I am aged 7 years old. It is the first musical instrument I have learnt to play. Band member Tom Aylett told me about the band and I am enjoying playing very much. I attend the band with my older brother David and twin Sister Isobel.

I live in Fulford and attend St Oswalds School, and like supporting my best football team Manchester United. There are lots of things I like to do such as, Swimming, Tennis Watching TV, playing on my Play Station 2. I also like helping my Dad, fishing, getting muddy, dogs, cats, cows, and finally watching football on TV.

David Metcalfe (Cornet) joined 2003

I have attended the Beginner's Band, for the last 4 weeks (it is February, 2003) and I am very keen on my lessons.

I am 9 years old and come along with my brother and sister (twins), Andrew and Isobel. Our friend, Tom Aylett, told us about the band as he plays with the Concert Band. I live in Fulford and go to St Oswald's School.

Isobel Metcalfe (Cornet) joined 2003

I have only just started lessons today (10.2.03), on the cornet.

This is the first instrument that I have learnt – I have been watching my brothers during their lessons – I am 7 years old.

I heard about the Beginner's Band through our friend, Tom Aylett, who plays in the Concert Band. I live in Fulford and attend St Oswald's school.

Jamie Oliver Pearce (Cornet) joined 2001
(Written by Jamie's mum on his behalf)

Jamie showed a great interest in learning a musical instrument at Dunnington Primary School, but lesson fees were very expensive, so we decided to try it at Rowntree's for a while to see if the novelty would wear off. He has never missed his lesson and loves going. Jamie has made lots of friends and really enjoys playing the cornet and getting to stay up late on Monday nights (rehearsal ends at 7.30 pm). Jamie's dad plays badminton for Nestlé and so is in the same building too, at the same time.

Jamie joined the Beginner's Band in July, 2001, just before the school holidays

195

and was loaned a silver cornet to practice during the holidays. He was thrilled to bits.

We have a great many family connections with the factory, all of his grandparents were employed there. Jamie also has an uncle and aunt who have worked for the company and his dad worked for a construction firm within the factory for a while. There is only Jamie's mum who hasn't work at the factory, however, mum did work for the Joseph Rowntree Foundation Trust, at the Navigation Road Warehouse office for a few years. Jamie's mum also plays badminton occasionally for Nestlé and used to go to the Judo Club (green belt), and the keep fit classes.

All our family, old and young, still go to the Nestlé family swimming club on Wednesday evenings, at the Yearsley baths. Mum goes most weeks and the family go in the holidays. Jamie's dad still plays a lot of badminton and is in the Nestlé 'B' team – soon to be moved out to Joseph Rowntree School, due to the dining block being sold off to Purey Cust Hospital. This is a sad ending for a friendly club with friendly familiar faces and people.

Jamie started on an old, scratched silver cornet in the summer of 2001, he was given a better silver cornet 1 year later and got a wonderful new cornet at Christmas, 2002. He now likes making up music along with his sister's electric guitar music – good job mum is deaf and can turn the volume down with hearing aids. Hopefully, at the new premises, Jamie's enthusiasm will continue to grow and develop.

Joanne Robinson (Solo Cornet) joined 2000

I am 35 years old and have 2 children – Daniel (10) and Lucy (4).

I went to Carr Infants and Junior School and then to Manor C of E Secondary School. I learned to play the recorder when I was at Junior School, and then the cornet and the flute. I played in the school band and orchestra.

After leaving school, I stopped playing all of them, but when my son was 7 I decided to go along with him, as he was learning, and I picked it up again – which lead to playing in the Beginner's Band. I play Solo Cornet and Daniel plays 2nd Cornet. I hope that by playing myself it will encourage my children to continue learning music.

At present, I am doing a course for computers. We always enjoy the concerts.

Charlotte Seaman (Cornet) joined 2002

I am 8 years old and attend Woodthorpe Primary School.

We had a music teacher come into our school, he brought some brass instruments for us to try. So I kept nagging my mum about wanting to play one. Mum asked about how much it would cost and if we needed to buy an instrument.

One of mum's friends told her about Nestlé Rowntree Band and so I came along to try an instrument and began playing the cornet.

I am not very confident at reading music, but I'm getting there. I played in the Christmas Concert and really enjoyed it. My family came to watch me. It was great being up on stage.

The only other time I have been on stage is with the choir at school and when I was in a pantomime for the Church. I also attend gymnastics and girls football and brownies, but I love playing in the Band best of all.

Melanie Seaman (Cornet) joined 2003

I have only just started to learn to play the cornet with the band.

I have never played a brass instrument before, but decided to learn after listening to my youngest daughter practice, and watching her play in the concert at Christmas. I religiously listen to her practice every Monday and ferry her in the car from Woodthorpe, where we live.

I am married with 2 children, both girls, one 10 and one 8 years old. I work part-time as a sales consultant for a major carpet retailer. I am also a Rainbow and Brownie Guider, where I help to run both Rainbows and Brownies at Acomb Methodist Church, every Wednesday, during school term times. I now also help to train girls football with the York City Girls Team.

The first instrument I was taught how to play was the recorder, I then went on to play the treble recorder. When I started senior school I started to learn the classic guitar, but was never very good at it.

My youngest daughter is helping me with the cornet and teaching me to play. I am now practicing with her at home. When we attend band practice every Monday it is just like one big family.

Daniel Taylor (2nd Cornet) joined 2000

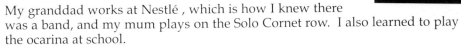

I am 10 years old and I go to Carr Junior School, and live in Acomb.

I started playing in September, 2000, and I also learn at school with the City of York Music Service. I have a lesson on my own with Mr Derek Warley.

My granddad works at Nestlé , which is how I knew there was a band, and my mum plays on the Solo Cornet row. I also learned to play the ocarina at school.

My favourite football team is York City and my favourite players are Lee Nogan and Alan Feltis (who is the football keeper for York at Bootham

Crescent). My favourite subjects at school are ICT (Information and Computer Technology) and Art. My cousins can play the cornet and the piano. My favourite hobbies are fishing and football.

Philip Taylor (1st Trumpet) joined 2002

I originally started learning to play the cornet in January, 1998.

I had music lessons at Wigginton Primary School, once a week.

In September, 1999, I moved to Joseph Rowntree School, where I continued my music lessons once a week. The very same month that I started secondary school, I joined the school training band. Practices were after school on Tuesdays.

In the summer 2000, I bought a new instrument – a trumpet (similar to a cornet, but slightly longer). In September, 2002, I tried out both the Beginner's Band and the then 'B' Band, before eventually deciding to settle with the Nestlé Rowntree Beginner's Band, to help to improve my playing standard before I progressed to the more advanced bands.

If I were to offer advice on playing an instrument it would be to keep at it and never give up.

SECTION 2

Behind the Stand

Associate Members

Mick Castro (Committee Member) joined 2002

I am the father of Leo who is a trombone player with the Senior Band.

I was elected onto the committee in 2002 and am pleased to be with the band as a supporter during their Centenary year. I was once a young member of the band during the early 60's, when I played cornet for a couple of years.

Liz Stamp (Treasurer) joined 1990

I became involved in the Nestlé Rowntree Band through my husband Kenneth (Ken) who plays Solo Trombone in the Senior Band. Until I met Ken, I did not know anything about brass bands or their music.

Over the years I have been 'educated', enjoying both music and the social side of the band. I have been treasurer for the last 2 years, which gives me more involvement with the band.

Margaret Mackintosh (Librarian) joined 1990

I was born and have spent the greater part of my life in York, working first as a Tax Officer and later as a Primary School Teacher. My father and his sister were amateur musicians all their lives, but I did not inherit their talent and I have never played a brass instrument.

Towards the end of 1990 I was asked if I would temporarily act as secretary to the band. That was the start of 12+ years of supporting and working for the band. I joined as Associate Member and continued as a member of the committee in various capacities. I brought up to date and maintained records of the Uniforms and Instruments and arranged a valuation of the Instruments (free of charge!)

I became Treasurer just after the take-over by Nestle and was instrumental in ensuring that the Band would thereafter be regarded as a separate entity from the factory, by de-registration from V.A.T, and preparation of our own accounts, including entering the instruments as assets of the Band.

When I became Librarian, the library was in the process of being computerised and I have continued this work – improving the database, checking entries and entering new pieces. We have about 2000 pieces of music plus the Concert Bands' and some very old un-catalogued and manuscript music.

I also collated and listed all our archive material. It made me appreciate the dedication of many bandsmen over the years, the pleasure they have given with their music and I am proud to be a member of that organisation.

SECTION 2

Behind the Stand

Past Members

Kirsten Smith (ex-2nd Cornet) 1997 – 2002

In 1993, at the age of 8, if asked whether 20 years later I would still be playing the trumpet – I am unsure if the answer would have been yes. The trumpet wasn't an instrument I had considered playing, but, at that time, my primary school (Headlands in Haxby) only offered brass instrument tuition.

At Joseph Rowntree school, in 1996, I joined the swing band, the concert band and the brass group. While a member of the swing band, I toured France, the highlight of this tour was playing at EuroDisney, in Paris.

Outside school, I played at York Music Centre, where I was a member of the York Area Schools Senior Concert Band (YASSCB). With YASSCB I participated in a tour of Canada and played for Queen Elizabeth, the Queen Mother's 100th Birthday Celebrations.

Looking for a new challenge I joined Rowntree Junior Band in 1997, alongside my Dad. I spent a happy year in that band before being asked to join the senior band. I played on the back row for 2 years.

Being a member of Nestlé Rowntree Band has presented me with many opportunities – the strangest of these was standing on the roof of York Minster, one dark night, in the middle of winter, playing in the Millennium 'Bells and Brass' Concert.

I am now 18 years old and I have left York and moved to Wales where I am a student at Aberystwyth University, studying Marine and Freshwater Biology. Here, I am a member of the Aberystwyth Silver Band and I play on the front row of the cornet section. I'm enjoying the change from Nestlé Rowntree Band yet, hopefully, will be back playing with them in the summer.

Sarah Joy (ex -2nd Cornet) 2000 – 2002

I started learning the cornet in 1995 at primary school, because my dad has a local wind band, which he wanted me to be a part of.

Nestlé Rowntree Band was the first brass band I had played in, as I was only 12 when I joined. I began going to training band in around March 2000 and moved into the Senior band in the September of 2000.

I passed my Grade 5 in the July, 1999, the year before joining the band. I joined at the same time as Kirsten – we had moved through the ranks together.

I had, and still have (hopefully) lots of friends at Nestlé Rowntree Band. I played at 2 area contests, while I was at Nestlé Rowntree Band. After the first one we got promoted to the Championship Section – this was a real achievement to me. My favourite contest was probably Hardraw Scar, in 2002, (this was the first Hardraw Scar since the Foot and Mouth Crisis), we won (every prize) – Best March, Best Hymn, Best Overall (for playing Carnival Overture) and also, therefore, claimed best conductor.

I currently attend Barbly High School – near Selby and I went to Barlby Hilltop CP School.

Martin Overton (ex Bass Trombone, 2nd Eb Bass) 1978 – 1988

I learned to play Flugel Horn and Trombone when I was 11/12 years old with Cockerton Band, Darlington, which only lasted 3 years. I attended the Darlington Grammar School, and my parents were violinists.

I took early retirement in 1993 aged 50 and now do gardening work and I have always been interested in sport. When I came to live in York as I was to be married, I played rugby for York Railway Institute, whilst playing with the Rowntrees Band. I returned to Brass Banding in 1978 when my first son Neil started playing trumpet at Tadcaster Primary School at the age of 7 years old.

We both joined Rowntrees Junior Band in 1978 I progressed to the Senior Band playing the Tenor and Bass Trombone, and also Eb Bass. Neil progressed to Principal Cornet in the Senior Band.

My second son Gareth followed Neil into the Training Band then progressed to Solo Horn with the Senior Band. These were very enjoyable years and I stopped playing around about 1988 when Neil and Gareth moved on to University.

My Wife, Pat and I were involved at times, on the Band Committee in various capacities.

Eleanor Guest (Trombone) 1994 – 1998

I started playing the Trombone at the age of 10 in 1994 when my brother, Richard (who was second cornet in Rowntrees at the time) brought me home a band trombone to try. I started with the Training and Junior Bands – moving to 2nd Trombone in the Senior Band in about 1996 to play alongside Ken, under Derek Warley and Chris Hirst. In my time in York, I also played in Orchestras including the York Area Schools Symphony Orchestra, Yorchestra, and the National Children's Orchestra.

In 1998, I moved with my family to Gloucestershire, where I have been playing Principal Trombone with the Cinderford Band, and studying under Brett Baker (the current Principal Trombonist with Black Dyke). I have continued my orchestral playing with the Royal Forest of Dean Orchestra, Gloucestershire Youth Orchestra and the Cotswold Symphony Orchestra. I also started playing with the Gloucestershire Youth Jazz Orchestra and now play with many big bands and smaller groups in the area.

I am currently in a gap year – I've just come back from backpacking around New Zealand and Australia, and in September I'll be moving back up North to read pharmacology at Leeds University, and to continue with all of my musical activities!

Brian Bousfield (Cornet) 1949 – 1986

Memories of the Rowntree Band

My first contact was in 1948 when the then conductor of the band was Les Lambert of New Earswick. He was, what we would today call, the brass peripatetic teacher. His school visits were, I think, restricted to Joseph Rowntree School; visiting every Friday (the school also had a visiting string teacher). Although he gave individual teaching his main objective was forming the school brass band, consisting during my time of 4 Cornets, 1 Flugel Horn, 1 Tenor Horn, 1 Euphonium and 1 Trombone. (Cornet – two Pawson brothers whose father played in the Rowntree Band, Trevor Bousfield and Gareth Lloyed, Flugel – Brain Bousfield, Tenor Horn – Frank Dawson, Euphonium – John Marshall. With the exception of the Trombone player the rest joined the Rowntree Band).

Les Lambert was in his day an excellent cornet player and came from an established brass band family. His love of brass band music and skill of interpretation gave his students a life time foundation, I personally was very much influenced by his knowledge.

He encouraged his young players to experience the principle chairs in each section whenever the opportunity presented itself. John Marshall and Frank Dawson for example were being schooled in the euphonium and tenor horn positions. Les also taught a young cornet player, Peter Mortimer, who was being schooled for principle cornet. Peter kept this position for many years and proved to be, as his teacher before him, one of Britian's finest players.

Les formed a young brass band quartet (1st cornet Peter Mortimer, 2nd Trevor Bousfield, tenor horn Frank Dawson, euphonium John Marshall), they were all 14 years old with the exception of Peter who was 16. I recall the quartet competing at the Home Firth Open Quartet Contest in 1950; I think they were very creditable placed about half way, say 12 contestants.

At the brass band culture of contesting, Les was an advocate and would encourage excellence in individuals in addition to group playing. My first experience of solo contesting was when Les organised a slow melody contest amongst his Joseph Rowntree pupils. We were all tutored individually prior to the contest, which was held in the school assembly hall. It took place after school on a Friday afternoon, the adjudicator positioned behind a mobile school blackboard. The winner (twin brother Trevor) was awarded with a medal. I was pleased to come second but as with all competitions, to lose is more difficult to cope with. This had an adverse effect on at least one instrumentalist, which was a great shame; he potentially was an excellent player.

Competing with the Rowntree Band had its moments when just coming second or third was a major achievement; at the time no doubt we thought we were robbed. Anyone who sat-in when Les Lambert rehearsed for a contest would appreciate the skill in which he, not only interpreted the music but also disguised as much as possible exposed areas; bass players, for example, who had great difficulty in holding sustained notes of equal volume without going out of tune. As I recall the words 'dive bombing' was not infrequently used – Bass trombonist who derived great pleasure from rasping – horn and baritone tuning. Les would have to re-tune some instruments at every rehearsal, in particular the day of the contest. As a young performer I had never before experienced a conductor who after a contest would often say 'you're pulling my arms off'.

Band vibrato was not controlled as is the case today, you developed on techique and stuck with it. There was a beautiful lip vibrator reminiscent in sound to string instruments, the Harry James hand vibrator favoured by dance band players and lastly the head shaking method; the Rowntree Band had them all.

I have had three separate periods of playing with the Rowntree Band, my first ended when I was 16 (1952). My father was a dance band musician and it seemed natural to do the same but there was a big problem, brass band players wanted nothing to do with dance band players; they were the opposition. This meant both Trevor and I had to choose between the two and dance bands won the day.

In 1957 we received our National Service call up papers. We were both fortunate in being able to join the Royal Signals band for the whole two year period. We were walking in the footsteps of Peter Mortimer, principal cornet of the Rowntree Band; he had just completed his two year stint with the band.

After the Royal Signals Trevor and I came back to York and found that Rowntree band were now not averse to having dance band players in their ranks. Teddy Pratt, one of the finest big band lead trumpet players in the district, was bumping-up at Rowntrees. Trevor and I attended band rehearsals as time permitted, this must have been the strongest and sweetest cornet front line of the day – Peter Mortimer on principle with the support of three big band trumpet players.

Unfortunately in 1961 a collapsed lung brought my brass playing days to a premature end, and to encourage my interest, Les Lambert (approved by committee) offered me the assistant conductor position. This entailed attending rehearsals, watching and listening as he trained the band. My conducting time was extremely limited and after a short period I left but not for the last time. After Rowntrees I took up the string bass and went back into dance bands.

My third period with the Rowntree Band occurred in the mid 80's when Trevor was conductor. Although I then worked in the midlands during the week I would come home in time to attend the Friday night rehearsals. My wife and I would also support the band when competing. I was for a period of about two years persuaded to play 3rd Cornet; I thoroughly enjoyed the experience even though it perhaps was not wise.

On one occasion when Trevor was rehearsing the band for a radio York concert we spoke about the rhythmic phrasing which brass bands traditionally, even today, have great difficulty in interpreting. To use a non-musical description they make syncopations sound corny. As a result of this conversation I took my string bass along to rehearsals and played the 'B flat' part. It was decided I would play for the concert – history was made that day but it was kept a secret.

In 1986 when Trevor was 50 a carved wooden bowl was presented to him at a band barbeque; not only did they present their conductor with a bowl but they generously included an identical model for his identical twin brother. It is a much treasured possession and brings back wonderful memories of my days in the Rowntree Cocoa Works Band.

John & Beverley Millson (Cornet/Soprano & Horn) 1973 – 1995 & 1991 – 1995

John first joined the band at the age of 7 in 1973 in the Training Band, after learning to play the Cornet at Bishopthorpe Junior School. He was taught in the Training Band by Mr Peter Mortimer.

John has left and rejoined the band on numerous occasions, finally leaving the band in 1995. Throughout his banding career he has always played Cornet, Solo Cornet and more lately as Soprano Cornet.

Beverley (Bev) met John when they both played cornet at the same school brass band. Bev and John both played in Ebor Brass, and then joined Rowntrees together. They both played in Rosyth in 1985 for the commissioning of H.M.S York.

John and Bev left the band, and in 1989 they married, rejoined the band in 1991, Bev played 2nd Horn whilst John played Soprano. They went to Ballerup in Denmark in 1993 to a music festival to join Baldur Band in an exchange visit with Rowntrees.

John left the band in 1995 to further his educational studies and Bev later in the year to have their first baby "Jessica". John and Bev now have two children, Jessica and Holly, which take up most of their time, but would like to stay in touch.

Thank You

John and Bev.

Daniel Gregg (Cornet, usually 2nd Cornet) 1991 – 1996

Lived in Copmanthorpe and went to Tadcaster Grammar School. I started learning Trumpet/Cornet at the age of 9 or 10 years, was taught by various teachers at school (including Chris Hirst), and then had private lessons from Ted Pratt, who introduced me to Rowntree Brass Band.

I started playing with the Junior Band in around 1991/1992, then graduated to playing with the Senior Band in 1993, playing 3rd and 2nd Cornet. I played with the Senior Band for about 3 years, and went on the band trip to Denmark in 1995. During this time we did various contest including the Areas, Durham League, Hartlepool, Murton, Hardraw Scar and Whit Friday Marches. We did many concerts including the Rowntree Theatre.

I have also played in Tadcaster Grammar School Concert Band and Orchestra, played in 'Pit Ochestra' for shows and learned to play piano. My Dad (David Gregg) plays with the Junior/Concert Band, and has also played with the Senior Band in the past on Trombone.

I now play 2nd Cornet with Greggs Bakery Brass Band, a Championship Section Band based in Newbiggin-by-the-Sea, in Northumberland, competing in various contests across the country, having done the National Finals (2nd Section) twice and worked under a number of professional conductors, such as Jimmy Shepherd, Ian McElligett and Gary Cutt.

I did BA (Hons), and a Diploma in Town Planning at Newcastle University, and now work for a professional town planning company in Newcastle City Centre, and I live in a suburb of Newcastle.

Whilst at University I played with the Newcastle University Jazz Orchestra.

Ian Bristow (Trombone) 1991(approx) – 1997

I learned to play in Harrogate Salvation Army and played in a number of Salvation Army bands, including Bradford Temple, Thurso and Chalk Farm. Between 1968 and 1971, when I was working at Sowerby Bridge Grammar School, I played with Friendly Band.

I moved back to Harrogate and in early 1972 joined the recently formed Harrogate Band. I have played in the Harrogate Band ever since but for several years I also played with York Railway, then Rowntrees and then Crystal Palace Band.

During the time I played with Rowntrees we had two memorable trips to Ballerup, Copenhagen.

Trevor Collins (Bass) 1977 – 2000

I started playing aged 11 at Okenhampton Silver Band, playing Cornet and rose to Repiano when I left to join the RAF.

At 16 during my RAF Career I played Cornet with various voluntary bands (part timers) at RAF Bassingbourn (Herts), RAF Sylt, RAF Wilderirath (Germany), RAF Watton (Norfolk) then switched to Tuba at RAF Sealand (Chester).

The voluntary band declined and I played for a short while with Bury-St-Edmunds British Legion, and came up north and started with Rowntree Mackintosh in 1977 and acted for a short period as secretary, then in 1984 I took over from Ray Rochester as Chairman for 13 years. After an accident I left Nestle Rowntrees, and I am currently playing with the Concert Band, the Holbourne Quintet and any one else who will have me.

Neil Overton (Cornet/Baritone/Euphonium–All Principal) 1978 – 1998

I learned to play the Trumpet at the age of 7 _ at Riverside School in Tadcaster, under Ken Jackson (peripatetic teacher). By the age of 8, Dad (Martin) had me in the training band under Peter Mortimer/Charlie Lund.

Before long I was on the back row in the days when we practiced after the table tennis club above the gym, and had to set out the long wooden music stands. I think by around 12-14 I was principal under the great Trevor Bousfield. We went to Dijon on an exchange, did radio Leeds and loads more. We played for Prince Charles at the opening of the York's Jorvik Centre.

I think we were on listen to the Band once after a stint at Sherburn-in-Elmet band (now Samuel Smiths). I returned but with a deeper voice, and tried my hand a Baritone, then Euphonium and eventually gave up for University. I played as a guest occasionally on and off but now have stopped altogether.

Piano, Guitar and a Teaching Career took over for most part, Dad (Martin) and brother (Gareth) were always there together. Names I remember are Ted, Frank, the Lunds, Rochester (Liz), Derek (Low?), Trevor (Bass), the Stamps – Ken, Keith and sister.

Kev Burbidge (3rd Solo Cornet) 1985 – 1989

I first learned to play cornet with a band from over the river (York Railway Institute) back in 1972. Learning to play cornet happened purely by accident. I was originally having Judo lessons in the gymnasium next door. My Mum bumped into a work colleague from the Glassworks (Albert Smith) who suggested that I should come along to the beginner's band on a Monday night and have a go. This was to be the start of a hobby that allowed me to play with many bands and orchestras both in the UK and Europe.

After joining the beginner's band in 1972, I progressed quickly to the junior band in 1973 and then through the ranks and finally finished up in my usual position of 3rd man down on the front row cornet section. I continued to play for the junior band until 1978 before progressing to 3rd cornet of the senior band. Once into the senior band it was not long before I was to take up my usual seat of 3rd man down on the front row and this was where I was to remain until 1984 when I left York Railway to play you guessed it 3rd man down for Askern Colliery Band. This transfer was to be short lived (10 months) with travel and work commitments impacting heavily on my playing.

It was this point that I joined Rowntree band in 1985 to play my usual position of 3rd man down on the front row. This was where I was to spend the next 4 years until work commitments were finally to halt my brass banding. This was a very hard thing to give up, rehearsals 2 nights a week, concerts as and when on weekend, it was a shock to the system not to play but a decision I had to make. My decision to leave the band was not an easy one but, a band requires players that are dedicated and can give 100% commitment. I was unable to give this level of commitment and thus regarded myself as being unfair to the other players in the band to stay.

Word spread fast that I wasn't playing and a call from Phil Carter at Kirby Moorside Band was to get me playing for a further 18 months, rehearsing on a Sunday evening until 1990 when my shift pattern changed to include Sunday working.

From the early '80's I was also spending a considerable amount of time playing Trumpet for dance bands and concert bands, which was an escape from the regimental structure of brass bands and an insight into a different style of music. In 1987 I was asked by a work colleague to play with a concert band from Barnsley, I explained that playing was difficult due to my shift patterns, but he said that this was not a problem and I could play as and when I could. This was to prove very amicable and 16 years later I'm still playing for the Barnsley Cooperative Concert Band.

Today I am Managing Director of my own Electrical Contracting Company working in York and surrounding area. I currently play trumpet for Barnsley Cooperative Concert Band, Ashton on Mersey Show Band and occasionally Halifax Symphony Orchestra.

H Humphrey (Trombone) 1927 – 1974

I would like to say how pleased I was to meet you and wish you with your project. I cannot add much to that which we discussed.

Started playing at school in 1924, and joined Rowntrees Coco Works Band in 1927. I was appointed secretary in 1936 and retired from the band in 1974.

Jenny Wilde (Reeder) (Tenor Horn – 1st) 1962/3 – 1971

My name is Jenny Wilder (Reeder). I joined the Rowntrees Band in about 1962 or 63, when I was 12 or 13 years old. I was the only girl among all the men and boys. We used to do lots of concerts and contests, Scarborough every year and Flamingo Park Zoo. I remember well, Belle Vue in Manchester was a big contest venue and remember going to London for a big contest in 1967 or 68, which was exciting. Pauline Stamp was with us by then along with her Dad and Brothers so I had some female company.

The band was a big part of my life, and I met my husband in it, Frank Wilde, his brother-in-law Derek Bilham and his father Len Bilham, were in it and dragged him along. We've been married 31 years.

I started playing cornet taught by my brother Mick Reeder, who plays trumpet and runs the York Concert Band. I moved on to Tenor Horn and played 1st part alongside Len Bilham on Solo. I left the band in 1971 to marry. I have ventured into banding since, playing with Malton White Star, but have given up again.

I went to the old Knavesmire Secondary School in 1961-65, then worked for Shepherd Building Group till 1975, when I had my 1st child Daniel. I had a daughter Amy in 1978. My Dad played with the old City Band in the 50's based in Blossom Street. His name was Charlie. I work for Tesco, Clifton Moor on the checkouts, and I've been there for 14 years. I've just got over Breast Cancer hopefully! So am enjoying being alive.

I remember Ernie Dobson, Reg Lawler and Dougie on Bass, Dave Wilde (no relation), John Henry, Nick Falconer – Drums. Ted Pratt, Ray Stamp, David Oakes, Steve Ashton – Cornets. Harry Wreghit – Flugel, Derek Bilham, Ken Stamp – Trombones, Euphonium - Ted Sutton, Bill Stamp. Horns - Len Bilham, Me, Dennis Stamp.

Bill Gilpin LTCL (Conductor) 1982 – 1983

I was an Army Bandmaster at the Junior Bandsman School, Strensall, when I was first involved with the Band. After retiring I conducted the band as a deputy on a couple of occasions. As a woodwind player I had very little connection with Brass Bands.

Whilst at Kneller Hall my Brass Band March 'Painswick Beacon', was awarded fourth place by the illustrious Harry Mortimer. He had written on the conductors score "where is the solo cornet part?"

I currently conduct 'York Concert Band' and live in the City.

Congratulations to Nestle Rowntree Band on their 100 years.

Iain Hasnip (Cornet & Baritone) 1985 –1995

I joined the Band in 1985 age 10 and the senior band three years later. I progressed through the ranks from 3rd to 2nd then solo cornet before switching to first baritone.

I left the band in 1995 when I moved to Edinburgh for University. I graduated from Edinburgh in 2000 with a Masters Degree in Physics. I have since been living in London where I am in the final year of my training to become a Chartered Accountant.

I have many happy memories of playing in the Rowntrees Band, notably winning the area championships two years in row, and the two trips to London for the national finals, not to mention the two trips to Denmark!

I am very grateful to all the members of the band for their friendship and for making those years of my life so enjoyable. From them I learned a lot about music and a lot about life.

David Bancroft (2nd Cornet/2nd Trombone)
1983 – 1988

I was born in Rochdale in January 1950 and now see myself as rapidly heading towards senior citizenship. I started playing when I was about 12 years old, and was taught by Stan Sheasby, who founded and ran his own band 'Ashworth Band', which is still in existence and the band is still rehearsing in Stan's premises. Stan now is in his 90's. When registered Ashworth is a fourth section band, but I believe for most of its time the band has been unregistered.

Since leaving Rochdale when I was 18 to go to University, I have only played with York Bands, first with Rowntree's in 1983 – 1988, under the baton of Trevor Bousfield and Howard Bousfield.

Then when my two sons showed initial interest I introduced them to Brian Henderson at Ebor. While Brian was teaching them I renewed my interest and I played with Ebor from 1995 for about two years. Neither of my two sons continued for more than 2/3 years and decided along with another Ebor player (John Freeborn) to join York Railway Institue. Why York Railway and not back to Rowntrees? There are probably three reasons:

1. Practice nights at Ebor and Railway Institute allowed us to attend both

2. My playing ability didn't match the then standard at Rowntrees

3. My ability to turn up to rehearsals/engagements was limited (family of 4, full time job and wife also working part-time evings)

I have been at York Railway Institute for about 4 years, with the last year taking on duties of secretary. I fully acknowledge that my playing abilities are limited and now play 2nd Baritone (but still remains an enjoyment).

While I was at Rowntrees I did have a spell on committee, Ray Rochester was chairman for a while, then Trevor Collins, Keith Morton was Secretary and I was Treasurer.

J Bernard Hewitt (Conductor) Early 1970's

I conducted the Rowntree Band during the early 70's, at the time they were a second section band, and had not won prizes for some years. During my period as conductor we had firsts, seconds and thirds at various contest, and were very busy in the concert field.

I am a true "Yorkie", born within the sound of the Minster bells.

Studied the Cornet from the age of seven and eventually became principal cornet of the York Citadel Salvation Army band and Deputy Bandmaster of York and Scarborough bands. Was Bandmaster of the York Citadel S A band for ten years.

I studied under George Thompson and Sam B. Wood, conducted the Gomersall Mills Band and left the Rowntree Band to conduct a Championship section band.

Secretary of the Yorkshire Area of the National Brass Band Championships for 15 year; Geoff Whitham was the chairman. Secretary of the Yorkshire Area of the National Association of Brass Band Conductors.

I have very pleasant memories of my time conducting the Rowntree Band, and hold dear the friends I made during that period.

Darryl Rayner (Eb & BBb Bass) 1991 – 1999

I first learned to play a brass instrument at the age of 10, when I started on Cornet in 1977 at the local Saturday morning music centre in Rothwell, south Leeds. Over the years I have played cornet with Sprowston Junior Band (in Norfolk), York Railway Institute Band, and Northfleet Brass in Kent.

In 1989 I moved from Cornet to BBb Bass via 6 months on 2nd Baritone at York Railway Institute. In 1991 I moved to Rowntrees on BBb Bass and took park in the 2 visits to the Nationals in 1992 and 93.

At the end of 1994 I moved to Birmingham with work and joined the City of Birmingham Brass Band on Eb Bass. At around this time I also joined the Svengali Big Band on Tuba, a position I held for about 6 years.

I moved back to York, again through work, in 1998 and rejoined the Rowntree Band on Eb Bass, where I remained until the middle of 1999. At this point I had to leave due to other commitments. I have been a member of the City of York Scout Band since 1993 and activities with the Scout Band were just taking up too mujch of my time.

At the end of the 1999 marching season, I was persuaded to rejoin the York Railway Institute Band to play Bass Trombone for the 2000 Areas. I kept this position until the middle of 2002, when again, I had to leave due to having to commit too much time to the City of York Scout Band, and also to help some friends out in the Queensbury Scout Band near Bradford.

I am not currently playing with a Brass Band, but I am now the Brass Section head at the City of York Scout Band, as well as being one of the small team of musical arrangers in the band. I am also playing Tuba with Generation Groove, a Haxby based, Wind Band/Jass Band/Rock Band Fusion.

For the last 4 years I have also assisted with instructing the Bb Wind Band course at the British Youth Band Association's annual Training week in Somerset.

Peter Richardson (Soprano) 1969 – 2002 (with a big break in the middle)

I learned to play with the York City B. B, taught by Bob Colley at nine year of age, moved to York Railway Institute at the age of 14, prior to Ron Milners Soprano. Inspired by Laurie Bruce I moved to Rowntrees to play Soprano till the age of 28 when studies forced an early retirement.

Started playing seriously 20 years later with lower grade bands, and rejoined Rowntrees in 1999 on Soprano staying for 2 years.

Now aged 56 I have started conducting and training lower graded bands and adjudicating solo competitions.

Major Donald Carson MBE LTCL psm (Conductor)
1976 – 1979

Learnt to play Piano from aged 4, sang in choir from the age of 5 to 16. Became Army Bandsman (Oboe) in 1950. Bandmaster's Course at Kneller Hall 1960-3, were I was taught to play all wind band instruments (not Tenor Horn or Baritone!).

Was appointed Bandmaster of Gloucestershire Regt. in 1963 and posted to Scotland (Black Watch 1969), Director of Music King's Division, York – 1975 (badged PWO regt. of Yorkshire), Director of Music Royal Army medical Corps from 1979-1984, then Director of Music Scots Guards from 1984-1988.

Retiring from Army became Head of Woodwind & Brass at Dulwich College South London form 1988-1997. My son Peter played Cornet with the band for a while (1978-1979). He became Senior Trumpet major of the Household Cavaliers before, in 1998 being involved in a very serious Road Traffic Accident, which has left him with severe brain damage.

Richard Guest (2nd Cornet) 1992 – 1996

At the age of 10 I started to play the trumpet, before switching to the cornet at 12, joining the Fielding Municipal Brass Band (New Zealand).

Our Family moved to York in 1992 and I joined Rowntrees. I had four great years with the band, playing many concerts, contests and joining the tours to Denmark in 93' and 95'. My sister, Eleanor, joined the band to play Trombone shortly before I left to attend University.

Since my departure from the band I have spent a couple of years travelling a host of Countries, and am now settled back in the Central North Island (Doforua), New Zealand. I am employed as a forest ranger for the largest forestry company in New Zealand, Carter Holt Harvey.

I am still playing the cornet, but not with any band at the present time. Most of my spare time is taken up outdoor, be it, tramping, mountain biking, fishing, scuba diving, snow-boarding etc.....

David Oakes (Cornet & Euphonium) 1958 – 1987

As a pupil at Archbishop Holgate's Grammar School, Lord Mayors Walk, York, I had lessons with Leslie Lambeth on how to play the Trumpet. I started at the age of 12 years on an old Trumpet which cost £8, and had to be cleaned with Duraglit each week, as it had no laquer coating. It didn't seem to want to produce a note above top G either!

In quick time I played 2nd trumpet in the school orchestra and Les Lambeth, the conductor and bandmaster at Rowntrees Band, invited me to play in the band. It was the start of a long and happy association with the Rowntree Band in particular the banding generally.

Whilst I left the band in 1987 I still keep in touch with close friends who played in the band with me. In recent years I have played with the Harrogate Band-still on Euphonium. When I joined Rowntree Band, quite a number of players were employed at the factory in York – approximately half. I was an external player and always found it interesting that the principle cornet player, Peter Mortimer, worked for Terrys, the rival chocolate factory in the City.

I joined the police, The York City Police, in 1966 and, following the amalgamation of police forces in the early 1970's had to move around the North Yorkshire Area because of my career. That never stopped me attending the rehearsals, jobs and concerts. I must have travelled many miles over the years to play in the band, every one worth it.

I was the bands Treasurer for a number of years, when Peter Mortimer was the Chairman, and remember well our negotiations to obtain increases in annual sponsorship from the company. We had great time playing all over the Country and I remember the personalities and events with great affection.

Playing a brass instrument has been the greatest hobby to have, and I think of Rowntrees Band as 'my band'.

Edward Sutton (Ted) Snr (Tenor Horn)
1903 – 1955 approx.

My Grandfather (Ted Senior) was one of the founder members of the band. My father (Ted Junior) and Uncle John both joined very early in the bands life. My father died in 1992, but remained a member until his death as a player and librarian. Uncle John used to teach young members of the band.

My father was an avid brass band enthusiast and thought being a member of a band was a really great part of his life. He followed all brass band events whenever possible and encouraged young people to make playing an instrument an important part of their lives.

He was awarded an Honorary Life Membership of the National Brass Band Club, following 50 years service in the cause of brass bands, as was his father.

Stephen Outhwaite 1987 - 1992

I grew up in west Yorkshire in a place called Hemsworth. I started playing cornet at the age of 10, because I thought it would be easy, having only three buttons. Living in a mining town in the 80's, and being able to play cornet it was only natural that I would join one of the local colliery bands (there were three, although I can only remember the one that I played with.) I started playing with Frickley Colliery Youth band in 1984, and slowly worked my way up from third cornet, being promoted to the solo cornet line a month before I left the band when we moved to York in 1987. I was overjoyed at being invited to play with Rowntree Brass Band (I was still a child - They make chocolate – I think you get the picture)

Ok then, Band No 2, and I started on the back row again (I can remember being slightly disappointed, but at least this was the real band, not a youth band, and you could smell the chocolate all of the time when you practiced) The first concert that I can remember was the marching contest at Easingwold – I can remember this vividly because I didn't realise it was a competition until about 10 minutes before the event started. When we were marching back in West Yorkshire it was common to have several bands playing in the same procession – one at the start, one at the end and sometimes one in the middle (they were BIG marches – or maybe they just seemed big to a 14 year old.), and I can remember thinking that the procession in Easingwold must carry on for miles and miles if we are all going to get in line without drowning each other out. Once my brain caught up, I realised why the Tenor Horn player (I think his name was Trevor) had spent the best part of an hour with me and Lee (whose surname has escaped me) in the car park on the Friday before, trying to get us to march in time (if I'd had two left feet, it would have been an improvement)

To me, the contests were the best thing about playing in the band – the challenge of working over and over a piece until the collection of discordant harmonies and tantalising melodies that were punctuated with harsh (sometimes even brutal) dynamics were transformed into music that would make the hairs rise on the back of your neck, then taking your interpretation of the piece and displaying it to the rest of the Brass Band fraternity, spending the rest of the day listening to how the other bands interpreted the same piece – pure magic. I can remember Duncan (Beckley? – conductor at that time) laughing at me (although not unkindly) for not being too bothered when we won in Darlington once. Duncan, some of us didn't care that much about winning, for me it really was the taking part that mattered.

I left York in 1992 to go to university in Teesside, and stopped playing cornet soon after. I now live in Saltburn in Cleveland with my wife and two wonderful daughters, working as Payroll Manager for a large convenience store chain.

Oveleaf are two pictures which Stephen sent of the Band at Easingwold March Contest.

Glenn Stewart Kilburn (Euphonium 2nd)

I started to learn the euphonium at the age of 10. I was sitting on a wall listening to the village band practice when the then conductor of the band Charlie Lund came out of the band room to give me what I thought at the time was going to be a telling off, instead he frog marched me into the band room and promptly gave me a euphonium. By the end of practice I could almost play a c scale.(if only I could pick things up that quickly now). I stayed with Sherburn for nearly 10 years playing solo euph. I eventually left the band and joined The John Waddington Band on 2nd Euph. This was a step up the gradings from 4 section to 1st.

I remained with JW for a couple of years and then, as many people do when they discover nighlife, packed in.

10 years later my old mate Charlie called on me once again to join Sherburn. So there I was, back in Band. However it wasn't too long before I was ready for the heady heights of playing once again in the higher sections and therefore joined Asda Manufacturing Brass. This was ok for a couple of years but the band fell into decline and unfortunately became none contesting. I left Asda and joined Carlton Main Frickley Colliery Band on 2nd Baritone. I didn't stay too long with Carlton as family pressures were too high and the commitment of playing in top section were beginning to tell its toll (another band widow).

I left Carton and rejoined Asda but now under the name of South Milford Brass. This band was languishing in the 4th section and was in danger of disappearing altogether , however the band reformed and quickly went from 4th to 2nd section in successive years. I was happy enough at SMB but had always wanted to play for the York Railway Institute Band.(a fine organisation residing in York). It was at the march Contest (Easingwold) were I first heard the then 2nd section Rowntree Band. I was really surprised how good they were and what was even more apparent at the contest was the rivalry between the two bands (YRI and Rowntrees) York Railway had in the past been the more successful band and believe me they (YRI) were not happy about the progress Rowntrees were making. Several months later I gave my resignation to YRI and planned to join Rowntrees. YRI were most supportive of my decision to leave, right up to the point of them finding out the I was defecting to Rowntrees .(I was almost lynched that day).

I stayed with Rowntrees for 2 great years but again decided to retire. Not for long, I was playing for Barnsley Building Society within the month. I did a couple of contests for BBS but my technique was going and I decided enough was enough. So there you are, a brief summery of nearly 20 years banding . And by the way I have packed in, honest. well, who knows !

The Alan Sutton Story.
Family Ties:
Father: Johnny Sutton
Grandfather: Edward E Sutton founding member
Nephew of: Edward A Sutton, Len Fawcett, Edward Fawcett

As a young child it was family policy to learn the piano. By the time I reached the age of eight I was rebelling at spending all my time practising. I was then asked what instrument I wanted to play, eventually I decided on the trombone. Uncle Ted Sutton indicated that a trombone was lying idle at the band room. Dad asked the committee if it was possible for me borrow it. The committee agreed and that was the start of my life as a trombone player. As dad had been involved with brass instruments for many years he was my teacher.

After about three years the committee asked my uncle Ted Fawcett as to how I was progressing. After consulting dad it was decided that I was proficient enough to sit in alongside second trombone at practice. This is when my problems started. In those days brass band trombone music was written in either treble clef or alto clef and the tutorial books I had used were written in bass clef. At the first practice I explained this and his usual manner Wilf Medley came up with a formula so I could read it as base clef.

After a short time I would play at fetes like Dunnington, the Homestead in Clifton and concerts. Originally I did not play on the marches but would be at the venue to play for background music. One of the regular engagements was the Remembrance Day march for the Selby branch of the British legion where we would march them to the abbey play some hymns and reveille and the last post. I stayed with the band until I was about eighteen, I then changed over to dance band with dad at the De Grey Rooms playing second trombone. After about eighteen months the bass player left and as the first trombone player was a bass player he moved over and I took the first trombone chair. I played with dad until I was twenty. I then gave the trombone away as it was purely mechanical and I had to work very hard to please dad and my heart wasn't in it at all so I gave it up.

My music for the next year was with St Helens Church choir in St Helens square. I joined the choir when I was eight. I failed the entrance exam to the York Minster choir and it was suggested by Francis Jackson that I joined the church choir for experience. The organist and choir master was a Minster old boy and that's why this church was suggested. When I finally passed the entrance exam for the Minster song school it was decided I was two weeks too old so I stayed at St Helens I changed to the men's section singing alto at the age of fourteen and remained with the choir until I was twenty two. I gave the choir up as I didn't have time to go to choir practice.

On Friday nights at the De Gray rooms we would play 8.00 pm until 1.00am. At midnight the pianist would play fifteen minuets of waltz and I would fiddle away on the drums. Then one Boxing Day night the drummer was ill and dad could not find a replacement. The drummer suggested to dad that he let me do the job. Dad could not do anything else but agree as it was me or nobody. At the end of the night the pianist congratulated me on keeping good tempo and getting my bass drum and hi –hat in the right place. I told dad this and I suggested I might buy a drum kit; his reply was that it was up to me. So I bought a cheap drum kit and started practicing and watching dad's drummer. After a year I shared the drumming in dad's band with another drummer that could work Wednesdays and Fridays so I did the Saturday nights. In 1963 the De Grey Rooms closed down and dad's band was augmented to fourteen players and we played at the Spa Ballroom Bridlington for a winter season. When the job at Bridlington finished it was the finish of the big band. Dad would not take less than nine players out on a job so I ended up gigging around the clubs and hotels in York and West Yorkshire until the new Layerthorpe WMC was built and I was resident there until coming to Australia in 1968. It took me about six months to get work here but once people heard me I had plenty of work.

Away from music I was educated at Canon A R Lee secondary school. I went on to the engineering dept of York Technical College for a year. I wanted to be an electrician but could not get employment. I ended up being an apprentice motor mechanic for five years in a small back street garage in Walmgate. When I qualified I moved to new Rover dealer in Piccadilly and was there until I came to Australia. With my Rover expertise I was employed by the New South Wales distributor for Rover the day I landed. I worked for them until 1975 when I left to start my own business. I retired in 2000 as I was finding it difficult to stand at the bench all day. I now do small repairs at home and spend three days a week as volunteer driver for the local community service transporting elderly people to see their loved ones in hospital and nursing homes.

Gareth Overton Horn (2nd, 1st then Solo) joined: 1980 (aged seven)

Left: 1988ish, but I spent time elsewhere in the meantime and I returned from time to time after 1988.

I first played with the junior band aged seven, with Peter Mortimer conducting, and I remember being such a beginner that the musical measure of a "bar" was a new concept to me. I wasn't making a great sound on the cornet and two rehearsals later Mr Mortimer persuaded me to try the tenor horn, and so began a big part of my formative years.

My older brother, Neil, was by then showing his star qualities as a cornet player, and my dad, Martin, was beginning his nomadic life amid the trombone and bass sections.

I have a world of memories from my times with the band, which were the times of my youth and its rites of passage. As with any such organisation there were politics and organisational disputes and all sorts of fallings-out, but as a boy I was blissfully ignorant of much of that and I look back now with almost unblemished fondness.

I was nurtured in the horn section by Liz Rochester, David Copley, and Derek Lowe, all wonderful companions, and I was conducted by, among others, Mr

Mortimer, David Walker, Trevor Bousfield, Derek Wharley, Keiron Anderson, Duncan Beckley and Ray Farr.

Some of my sharpest memories are from the time we visited Dijon in 1984. The conductor was Trevor Bousfield, whose amazing qualities as a musician I probably didn't fully appreciate at the time (and, incidentally, whose eldest son, Ian Bousfield, was to become one of the best trombonists in the world).

I can still hear, and see in my mind's eye, Trevor's arrangements of Ravel's Bolero, Rimsky Korsakov's Troika, the "Grandstand" theme tune, "Hello" by Lionel Ritchie and several others pieces, all of them exquisitely done. He had a wonderfully fatherly way of coaxing what he wanted from the band.

I also remember Mick Evans who was one of the big personalities in the fun we all had in France that year and, strangely, once fixed the Overton family vacuum cleaner.

I can't judge all these years later whether I was a shy, sweet boy or a precocious brat, but either way I have a lot to thank the band for.

While I was still in the junior band the Overtons emigrated to the Sherburn band, which became the Samuel Smith's Brewery band, but we soon returned to Rowntrees. In my late teens I jumped ship and joined Kippax Band, by which time I was also playing in the National Youth Brass Band, where I played top spot in the 15-strong horn section. I later conducted Cambridge University Brass Band for two years. In my early 20s I took up the trumpet, which I played in a York orchestra and a big band, and with the Yorkshire Wind Orchestra, coincidentally conducted by Keiron Anderson. Later I was privileged to play in some of London's wonderful amateur orchestras and bands.

Now, aged 30, I live in Brussels, where I'm a journalist. I still play the trumpet and the piano.

David Farmer 1992 – 1996

I was a member of the band between 1992 and 1996 and played the Eb Bass. I first started playing the instrument in 1988 at the age of 8 and studied from 1991 with Brian Kingsley of Opera North. My Sister Elizabeth was also in the band and also played in the Swinton & District Excelsior Brass Band with me before we went to Rowntrees. I left the band in 1996 to go and study at the Chethams School of Music in Manchester. Once I had finished my A-levels I went to study at the Royal Academy of Music in London. Whilst at the Royal Academy I worked with many famous groups and orchestras such as the Black Dyke Mills Brass Band, London Orphean Brass, RAM Brass Soloists, the London Pops Orchestra, Cast and was in the Orchestra for the Golden Jubilee Pop Concert at Buckingham Palace working with such artists as Sir Paul McCartney, Dame Shirley Bassey, Rod Stewart, Phil Collins, Joe Cocker and Brian May. I was also awarded the Vice-Principal's award for my final recital at the Royal Academy. Now in 2003 I am the Sales Executive for a company that provides music in schools and also professional musicians to work with children.

Elizabeth Anne Farmer Tenor Trombone 1994 - 1997

I started to learn to play the tenor horn at the age of 7 when I joined Swinton and District Excelsior Band, with whom I was a member for a number of years. I followed David, my brother, to the Nestlé Rowntrees Band in 1994 while studying for my A-levels at All Saints School in York. As well as playing in brass bands while at school, I played the French horn and the tenor horn in a number of wind bands including the North Yorkshire Schools concert band.

Since leaving school in 1997, I have played in brass bands across the country as my studies have led me to various universities. While studying for my physical geography degree at the University of Reading I was a member of the Reading Spring Gardens Band. Following this my studies took me to the University of Cranfield, Silsoe. After completing my masters degree in Geographical Information Management, I have recently decided to stay in Silsoe to undertake a PhD in the field of remote sensing and geographical information systems. After a break away from brass-banding I am currently enjoying a return to contesting, concerts and rehearsals with both the Ampthill and Hitchin brass bands.

David and Pat Pawson 2nd and 3rd Cornet respectively 1949 - 1951

We left the band in 1951 when the family emigrated to Australia.

After arriving in Australia, both of us resumed school and our father Harry, who played soprano cornet with the band, formed his own Tile Laying business. At the same time, he also built our own house, where our mum, who is now almost 94, still resides. After all dads' effort, he never enjoyed the fruits of his labour as he died in 1962 aged only 50.

Pat: After a brief association with the Yarraville and Kingsville Band, (now known as the Yarraville and Footscray) he never continued his playing career, mainly because Dad was too busy to play and therefore the inspiration was no longer there.

When he had finished his schooling, he joined father in his tile laying business and continued with this work until recently retiring. His passion is driving his 4 wheel drive cross country vehicle with his wife June (from Bromsgrove), and friends, to many places throughout Australia, in particular to remote bush camps and historic sites. He has enjoyed this pastime for many years and being self-employed, he regularly left his job and took off into the bush and desert area of Australia for weeks, and sometimes months at a time. He also enjoys riding pushbikes and walking.

David: Continued schooling for a while at the Footscray Technical College and was a member of their small band. I also played for a short period of time with the Yarraville and Kingsville band but gave up playing when the family moved well away from the district. After my schooling was finished, I commenced work with Australian National Airlines (now defunct) as an apprentice aircraft mechanic. After gaining some experience and engineering licences, I then moved to Hong Kong and worked for Cathay Pacific Airways for 20 very enjoyable years before retiring in 1991. Another passion of mine is Motor Cycle Road Racing. In my youth, I indulged in this sport for a few years until work forced me to give it up. As a competitor, I found this pastime to very exciting but there was occasional seconds of terror.

Shortly before retiring, I learnt to fly and following my return to Australia, bought my own aircraft (a Piper Arrow) so that I can go where I want, when I want. I have also built my own kit plane but I have not yet got around to getting it certified.

Leslie David Carter (BBb Bass) 1968 – 1970

I have been a member of the Malton White Star Band for fifty-two years and still practicing every week!! I am 62 years old and still going strong.

I was a member of Swinton & District Excelsior Band for 10 years and a member of York Raily Institute for 12 years. I was taught by Malton WSB bandmaster Mr Alfred Bogg (deceased) in 1950.

My grandfather, father, two uncles and two brothers have all been members of MWSB. My brother, Edwin Carter, is the current bandmaster and has completed 62 years in the band.

I attended Norton CP Boys School, now demolished. I also have a nephew in the MWSB.

To the best of my knowledge our family history in the brass band world goes back 150 years (approx.). The Malton WSB was previously known as the Malton Temperance Band and my grandfather was a member in 1899.

I was a blacksmith for 28 years before being made redundant and having two years on the dole. I eventually found a job at a bacon factory, for six years until it closed, making me redundant again and on the dole for a re endeavours from me and all the members of the MWSB.

Robert Melling Cornet 1987 – 1991

Robert was born in Plymouth,educated in York and moved to Glasgow in 1991 when he won a scholarship to study at the Royal Scottish Academy of Music and Drama. He gained a BA Hons and subsequently graduated with a Mmus performance degree in piano. At the Academy he won all the duo and accompaniment prizes including the principle's overall prize. His concerto performances include Shostakovich's 2nd piano concerto, Gershwin's Rhapsody in Blue and Jolivet's Concertino for trumpet piano and strings. Since entering the RSAMD he has performed regularly with various singers and instrumentalists as well as a soloist taking part in masterclasses with Roger Vignoles, Geoffrey Parsons,John Streets and Martin Isepp at the Britten Pears School.

He has performed throughout Britain including venues such as the Queen Elizabeth Hall, Wigmore Hall, Academy of St Martin in the Fields Auckland Palace Durham and extensively throughout Scotland. Robert has also worked with the Chamber group of Scotland,BT Scottish Ensemble,Paragon,the Royal Scottish National Orchestra,Cappella Nova and the John Currie Singers. He has performed in recital for radio 3 at the National Portrait Gallery and for Radio Scotland. He was awarded a commendation in the Maggie Teyte competition in Covent Garden and was chosen to perform in Graham Johnson's Song makers Almanac masterclasses and concert at St. John Smiths Square. Robert has given a recital tour of Iceland and regularly performs at the Festival International de Music et des Arts de Latour de France. He gave a voice and piano recital at the Louvre ,Paris for radio France and a recital in Hertogenbosch,Holland, repeated in Edinburgh and Glasgow performing a programme of contemporary Scottish music for solo piano and voice and piano.

Robert's opera experience includes work with Opera on a Shoestring, Perth festival opera, British youth opera,RSAMD,Co-operative Opera Galactic for the Edinburgh fringe and the Mannan Opera Festival. He has worked at the RSAMD and currently teaches piano at Glenalmond college Perthshire.

Peter Mortimer

I started playing with York City Brass in 1943-44. After showing promise, Herbert Humphrey asked me along to Rowntrees (they did not normally have youngsters).

The band had A Lambeth, Solo Euphonium, who left and went to St. Hilda's and his brother Les, who was Principal Cornet. Les later took over as conductor with assistance from his father, who was a top northern conductor of mining bands. We also had visits from J. Atherton and N. Ashcroft, top conductors and players. They had a big influence on my playing, as did T. Sutton and H. Wreghitt.

I started solo contesting and won many awards in the North of England, winning the North of England Slow Melody Championship, which included players from all the top bands.

In 1949-50 I was appointed Principal Cornet and remained so until I had to retire due to an ear problem.

In 1955 I passed the audition to play for the Royal Signals Band (a Major Staff Band), during my national service and did many broadcasts and some TV work. I was asked to join Black Dyke in 1962 but my wife did not like the area. In 1969 I played with W. Hargraves (Stanshaw-Sun Life) – they won Granada Band of the Year in 1970.

During this time I completed a Junior Coaching course with Mr G. Thompson who conducted Grimethorpe at the time. I taught brass at Ampleforth College Prep School and also took the Rowntree Junior Band and Players when we won the York and District Junior Band Awards for a number of years. I spent 18 years as chairman of the band – negotiating with the Company on financial issues, etc.

SECTION 3

Appendix

What's in a Name?

1903	Cocoa Works Brass Band
1905	Rowntree Brass Band
1906	York Cocoa Works Brass Band
1906	Cocoa Works Brass Band
1907	Rowntree's Brass Band
1908	Rowntree's Cocoa Works Prize Band
1910	Cocoa Works Prize Band
1910	Rowntree's Cocoa Works Prize Band
1919	Rowntree's Brass Band
1930	Rowntree's Cocoa Works Band
1966	Rowntree Works Band
1977	Rowntree Mackintosh Work Band
1990	Rowntree Brass Band
1999	Nestlé Rowntree Band

Conductors through the Century

1903	Anthony Lickley
1911	G.F. Lickley
1927	Wright Hainsworth
1932	George Walker
1945	Lesley Lambeth
1954	Harry Lawn
1957	Lesley Lambeth
1969	Gordon Pulleyn
1970	Johnny Sutton/Cyril Payne
1971	Geoffrey Brand
1973	Bernard Hewitt/Denzil Stephens
1974	Harry Lawn/J. Hewitt
1975	C. Hicks
1976	Capt. Don Carson/ Frank Renton
1977	Kenneth Jackson
1979	Leighton Rich/David Wood
1979	Geoffrey Whitham
1980	David Wood
1981	Capt. Phil Evans/Trevor Bousfield/ Bill Gilpin
1983	Bob Garrity/Peter Mortimer/Trevor Bousfield
1988	Duncan Beckley/George Thompson
1989	Ken Robinson/T. Walmsley/Chris Lawn
1990	Andrew Owenson/ Derek Warley
1998	Chris Hirst
2001	William Rushworth

Contests

1907	Crystal Palace Contest	2nd
1908	Malton Contest	4th
	Woodkirk Contest	5th
	Ilkley Contest	-
	Crystal Palace Contest	3rd
1909	Crystal Palace Contest	6th
1910	Crystal Palace Contest	2nd
1911	Crystal Palace Contest	4th
	Rothwell Contest	-
1912	Crystal Palace Contest	2nd
	Keighley Contest	3rd
	Pickering Contest	2nd
1913	Crystal Palace Contest	-
	Amorley Contest	-
	Keighley Contest	3rd
1914	Crystal Palace Cancelled	
1914 – 1919 – All contests cancelled due to The Great War		
1920	Selby Contest	-
1923	Selby Contest	-
	Kippax Contest	2nd
	Crystal Palace Contest (4th Section)	4th
1924	Crystal Palace Contest	-
1927	Crystal Palace Contest	-
1928	Ripley Castle Contest	1st March
		2nd Select
	Knaresborough Contest	3rd
	Crystal Palace Contest	-
1929	Driffield Contest	2nd
	Crystal Palace Contest	-
1930	Burley-in-Wharfedale Contest	1st
	Bridlington Contest	1st
	Crystal Palace Contest	3rd

1931	Selby Contest	
	Bridlington Contest	4th
	Crystal Palace Contest	-
1932	Crystal Palace Contest	-
1933	Burley-in-Wharfedale	-
	Crystal Palace Contest (4th Section)	-
1934	Crystal Palace Contest	-
1935	Belle Vue (Manchester) Contest – May	1st
	Belle Vue (Manchester) Contest – July	5th
	Crystal Palace Contest	-
1936	Belle Vue (Manchester) Contest – July	3rd
	Crystal Palace Contest	5th
1937	Belle Vue (Manchester) Contest	3rd
	Alexandra Palace (ex Crystal Palace)	-
1938	Belle Vue Contest	-
1939	Belle Vue Contest	-
1939 – 1945 – All contests cancelled due to Second World War		
1947	Yorkshire Areas, Huddersfield	5th
1948	Belle Vue Contest	2nd
1949	Filey Contest	-
1950	Yorkshire Areas	5th
	Belle Vue	£2 prize
1951	Yorkshire Area	5th
1952	Yorkshire Area	5th
1952	Yorkshire Area	5th
1957	York & District	1st
1958	York & District	1st
1959	York & District	1st
1960	York & District	1st
1961	York & District	2nd & 3rd
1962	York & District	1st
1963	Grantham Contest	2nd
	Kirbymisperton Contest	1st
	York & District	2nd
1965	York & District	1st & 2nd

1966	Area Contest (2nd Section)	2nd
	York & District	1st & 1st
	National Finals	
1967	Area Contest (2nd Section)	2nd
	National Finals	
1968	Area Contest	5th
	National Finals	
1973	Harrogate & District (1st Section)	1st & 2nd
1974	Yorkshire Areas (2nd Section)	
1976	Area Contest	11th
1978	Area Contest	6th
	YHBBA	2nd & 3rd & 8th
1979	Belle Vue	
1980	Area Contest	7th
1987	Peterlee Contest	1st
	Area Contest (3rd Section)	7th
	Skegness Contest	4th
	Nostell Priory Contest	
	Rossington Contest	1st
1988	North of England Areas (3rd Section)	1st
	National Finals	
1991	North of England Areas (3rd Section)	3rd
1992	North of England Areas (2nd Section)	1st
	National Finals	6th
1993	Durham League	2nd
1993	North of England Areas (2nd Section)	1st (promoted)
	Peterlee Contest	2nd
	National Finals	18th
1994	North of England Areas (1st Section)	Disqualified
1995	Durham League	2nd
	Camerons (Hartlepool) Contest	3rd
	North of England Areas (1st Section)	Demoted
1996	Durham League	3rd
	North of England Areas (2nd Section)	4th

1997	Durham League	2nd
	North of England Areas (2nd Section)	5th
	St Helens	4th
	Malton Entertainment	4th
1998	North of England Areas (2nd Section)	1st (Promoted)
	National Finals	14th
	Easingwold Marching Contest	4th
1999	North of England Areas (1st Section)	2nd & Best Basses
	National Finals	7th
	Malton Entertainment	2nd
2000	North of England Areas (1st Section)	4th
2001	North of England Areas (1st Section)	4th (Promoted)
	Brighouse March & Hymn	10th
2002	North of England Areas (Championship)	8th
	Malton Entertainment Contest	3rd
	Hardraw Scar	1st & 1st & 1st & Best Conductor
2003	North of England Areas (Championship)	5th

Sharon Lang

Sharon has completed the mammoth task of researching and writing this book. She has cajoled Band members to write up their potted biographies, she has read through all the minutes of countless meetings and prepared the book for printing. It falls to me now to thank her for this tremendous effort.

When we the committee discussed how best to mark our Centenary we began by looking at all the old photographs we had. Many had names attached but that was all. We had no details of the lives of these people. Sharon, by her efforts, has brought some of these names to life for us and by collecting the details from present band members she has ensured a written record for all future band members to gain inspiration from.

Reading through the history of our Band one is struck by the same problems occurring time after time but through it all, the Band has survived. Many of the members of the present Band remark on the friendliness of the people in the Band. This is a great tribute to all the Band members.

This book would not have been published but for the work of another person, Peter Wade. He joined the Band as a playing member for a brief period in 2003 but had to retire due to ill health. This did not stop him from devoting lots of energy to securing the Bands financial future by obtaining some very useful grants and also getting the Band registered as a Charity. The costs of running the band have risen enormously since we gained Championship status and the Band finances were such that we could not afford the costs of printing this book. Sir Donald Baron, a former Director of Rowntrees kindly made a donation towards the costs but Peter, our wizard with words, our guru of grant forms set about obtaining a further grant to cover the whole cost of the publication.

So to sum up I, on behalf of the Band, wish to record our thanks to all the members and retired members who contributed to the book, Sharon Lang who wrote the book, Peter Wade who got the money to publish the book and The Nestle Company for providing the grant to print the book.

Audrey Brown, Band Secretary.

INTO THE FUTURE - 2004

The book has focused on the history of the Nestle Rowntree Band since its inception in 1903. A further year has passed since we celebrated the Centenary of the Band. A year which has been very momentous in the Band's history so, before the book draws to a close, we should include brief details of what has happened to the Band this year.

Ronwtree Cocoa Works, the company that formed the Band in 1903, was a local company based here in York. Throughout the Band's History the Company had grown to become the major employer within the City with factories involved in Chocolate production throughout the U.K. In the 1980's the company became part of the multinational Nestle Company. Gradually decision making moved from York to the U.K. Headquarters in Croydon. There followed changes in priorities and emphasis to meet the demands of a global company.

The company continued to offer support to the Band but a major blow occurred when the Band Room was lost. The Band felt that it had a duty to the younger generation and any future members in and around the City of York to preserve and hopefully offer the Band a future of progress and not decline. We agreed that it was time to secure a new sponsorship deal reflecting our status as a York Band.

To this end in March 2004 the Band secured a new sponsorship deal with The Shepherd Building Group. Whilst Shepherd's is a multinational company it's Headquarters and roots are firmly centred in and around York.

The Shepherd Building Group has provided the Band with a new rehearsal facility it can proudly boast is one of the best band rooms in the country with ample storage facilities for our music and instruments.

2004 has been a momentous year for the Band. Engagements included a wonderful Concert to mark the change of sponsorship in the York Theatre Royal and an immensely successful run of the musical play – "Brassed Off" at the Theatre Royal. In the midst of all this some players resigned and a new Musical Director was appointed.

So we begin the next hundred years of our history with a very eventful year. The changes this year at some points threatened the very existence of the Band but we have come through and the set up is stronger for the struggle. We now have a flourishing Beginners Band, a Concert Band, steadily improving in its musicianship and a Senior Band looking forward to preserving it's title of North Yorkshire's premier band. Something that the Band and the citizens of York can be truly proud of.